THE TRUTH BEHIND OLD WIVES' TALES

THOMAS CRAUGHWELL
Illustrated by Marie Coons

Broadway Books • New York

Conceived, designed and produced by
EYE
276 Fifth Avenue
Suite 205
New York, NY 10001

Editor: Charles Clough
Cover design: Tamaye Perry
Interior design: Sheila Hart Design, Inc.
Copyeditor: Adam Sommers
Proofreader: Edwin Kiester Jr.

Publisher: William Kiester

Visit our website at www.broadwaybooks.com

Library of Congress Cataloging-in-Publication Data is on file with the Library of Congress

ISBN 0-7679-2188-7

Printed in China by Midas Printing International Limited.

10 9 8 7 6 5 4 3 2 1

For the young Carlsons—
Hilary, Matt, Melanie, Mark, and Eric—
who are too smart to believe that a dog's mouth
is cleaner than a human's.

CONTENTS

Introduction 11

Section One: A Dog's Mouth Is Cleaner Than a Human's, and Other Old Wives' Tales to Keep You Healthy

A Dog's Mouth Is Cleaner Than a Human's 16
It's Unhealthy to Hold Back a Sneeze 19
Listening to Loud Music Causes Deafness 21
Babies Who Suck Their Thumbs Will Have Buck Teeth 23
Reading in Dim Light Will Ruin Your Eyes 25
More People Commit Suicide Between Christmas and New Year's Than at Any Other Time of the Year 27
Toads Give You Warts 29
If You Cross Your Eyes, They Will Stay That Way 31
If You Go Outside With Wet Hair or Wet Feet, You'll Catch a Cold 32
Crack Your Knuckles and You'll Develop Arthritis 34

Section Two: If You're Carrying the Baby High, It's a Girl, and Other Old Wives' Tales About Pregnancy

If You're Carrying the Baby High, It's a Girl 38
If a Pregnant Woman's Face Is Puffy, She's Going to Have a Girl 41
If the Labor Is Difficult, the Mother Is About to Give Birth to a Boy 42
If the Baby Is Late, the Mother Should Take Long Walks 43
If You Crave Spicy Food, You're Having a Boy; If You Crave Sweet Food, It's a Girl 45
Voluptuous Women Were Built for Child-bearing 47

Section Three: Lightning Never Strikes the Same Place Twice, and Other Old Wives' Tales About the Weather

Lightning Never Strikes the Same Place Twice 50
No Two Snowflakes Are Exactly Alike 52
If a Groundhog Sees Its Shadow on February 2,
We'll Have Six More Weeks of Winter 53
People and Animals Behave Strangely during a Full Moon .. 55
A Red Sky in the Morning Means a Storm Is Coming 57
Arthritis Flares Up in Wet Weather 59
It Can Be Too Cold to Snow 61
Tornadoes Cannot Cross a River 62

Section Four: Swimmers Should Wait an Hour After Eating Before Going into the Water, and Other Old Wives' Tales About Sports

Swimmers Should Wait an Hour After Eating
Before Going Back into the Water 66
Golf Courses Have 18 Holes Because a Fifth of
Scotch Whiskey Contains 18 Shots 68
Spousal Abuse Reaches Epidemic Proportions on
Super Bowl Sunday 70
Magnets Heal Sports Injuries Faster Than
Conventional Medicine 72
It's Bad Luck to Change a Boat's Name 75
The Type of Baseball Bat a Player Swings Can Make
or Break His Career 76

Section Five: You Can Tell the Length of a Man's Penis by Checking Out His Shoe Size, and Other Old Wives' Tales of the Ways of Love

You Can Tell the Length of a Man's Penis by Checking Out His Shoe Size 80
Opposites Attract 82
Cold Hands, Warm Heart 85
Eating Powdered Rhinoceros Horn Improves a Man's Virility 87
After Sex, If a Man Washes His Penis with Aloe Vera, He Won't Contract Sexually Transmitted Diseases 90
Men Think About Sex Every Fifteen Seconds 92
Dog Meat Boosts a Man's Virility 94
You Can't Get Pregnant in a Hot Tub 96

Section Six: Walking Under a Ladder Is Bad Luck, and Other Old Wives' Tales to Keep You Safe

Walking Under a Ladder Is Bad Luck 100
If You Stick Your Tongue Out, You Will Absorb Millions of Germs and Bacteria 102
If You Kill a Cobra, Its Mate Will Come after You 104
Baby Snakes Are More Poisonous Than Adults 106

Section Seven: To Get the Marriage Off on the Right Foot, Carry the Bride Across the Threshold, and Other Old Wives' Tales of Marriage

To Get the Marriage Off on the Right Foot, Carry the Bride Across the Threshold 110
On February 29, a Woman Can Ask a Man to Marry Her 112
To See a Magpie Means You're About to Marry 114
Men Have One Less Rib Than Women 116
Throwing Rice at the Bride and Groom Brings Them Good Luck 117
Sleeping in Blue Sheets Makes the Bridegroom Virile 120

Section Eight: Water Goes Down the Drain in Different Directions Depending on Which Hemisphere You're in, and Other Old Wives' Tales About Running a Household

Water Goes Down the Drain in Different Directions Depending on Which Hemisphere You're In 124
It's Bad Luck to Kill a Ladybug 126
Club Soda Removes Red Wine Stains 128
Mistletoe Is an Antidote to Poison 129
It's Bad Luck to Kill a Bee 131
A Cricket in the House Is Good Luck 133
It's Bad Luck to Kill a Spider 134

Section Nine: Chicken Soup Is a Great Cold and Flu Remedy, and Other Old Wives' Tales About Food

Chicken Soup Is a Great Cold and Flu Remedy 138
Chinese Ginger and Spring Onion Soup Is a Great Cold and Flu Remedy 141
Wine Is Good for You 142
An Apple a Day Keeps the Doctor Away 144
Fish Is Brain Food 146
Carrots Are Good for the Eyes 149
Children Shouldn't Drink Coffee As It Will Stunt Their Growth 150
Boys Who Drink Coffee Will Be Beardless 152
Potatoes with a Greenish Tinge Are Poisonous 154
Cool Foods Are Good for a Fever 156
It's Dangerous to Eat Oysters in Months that Do Not Have an "R" in Them 158
You Burn More Calories Eating a Stick of Celery Than Are Contained in the Celery Stick 159
White Spots on Your Fingernails Mean You Need Calcium . . 160
Flat Ginger Ale Is Good for a Queasy Stomach 162
It's Safe to Eat Food Dropped on the Floor If You Pick It Up Within Five Seconds 163

Section Ten: A Severed Head Stays Alive for Several Minutes, and Other Old Wives' Tales About the Life of Crime

A Severed Head Stays Alive for Several Minutes After It's Been Separated from the Body . . . 166
It's Bad Luck to Buy a House Where a Murder Took Place . . 169
A Dog Can Smell Blood on a Murderer's Hands, Even Years after the Crime . . . 172
Burglars Check the Newspaper Obituary Page to See Who's Died, Then Rob the House While Everyone's at the Funeral . . . 174
If the Hangman's Rope Breaks During an Execution, the Prisoner Is Innocent . . . 176

Section Eleven: Chocolate Causes Acne, and Other Old Wives' Tales About the Human Body

Chocolate Causes Acne . . . 180
We Use Only 10 Percent of Our Brains . . . 182
We Are Taller Than Our Ancestors Were . . . 184
People with Red Hair Are Temperamental . . . 186
We're Only Six Degrees Away from Every Other Person on the Planet . . . 188
Shave Your Body Hair and It Will Grow Back Thicker . . . 191

Section Twelve: To Bring Good Luck, Knock on Wood, and Other Old Wives' Tales on How to Attract Good Luck and Avoid Bad Luck

To Bring Good Luck, Knock on Wood . . . 196
Break a Mirror and You'll Have Seven Years of Bad Luck . . . 197
Certain Lucky Numbers Come Up Again and Again in the Lottery . . . 199
Number 13 Is Lucky or Unlucky . . . 202
Number 8 Is Lucky in China . . . 203

7 Is the Perfect Number 205
Tuesday Is Unlucky 207
A Cat Aboard Ship Brings Good Luck 209
Wearing an Opal Is Unlucky Unless It Is Your Birthstone . . . 211
It's Good Luck to Hang a Horseshoe
Over the Door of a House 213
Friday the 13th Is Unlucky 215

Section Thirteen: Elephants Are Afraid of Mice, and Other Old Wives' Tales from the Animal Kingdom

Elephants Are Afraid of Mice 220
Ostriches Bury Their Heads in the Sand 222
The Most Poisonous Thing on Earth Is Polar Bear Liver . . . 223
Vampire Bats Suck Human Blood 225
Bees and Wasps Sense Fear 228
Opossums Play Dead to Fool Predators 230
Lemmings Commit Mass Suicide 231

Bibliography 233

INTRODUCTION

The basic fact about urban legends—those popular stories of stolen kidneys and alligators in sewers—is wonderfully simple: fundamentally, no urban legend is true. Old wives' tales, on the other hand, are a bit more complicated. Some are demonstrably false. Others are based on a seed of truth. But there are some cases in which the old wives were right on the money.

For example, generations have been nursed through colds and flu with a steaming bowl of chicken soup. In our skeptical age, most of us would be inclined to regard this old wives' remedy as ineffective but harmless, a little comfort food for the patient.

Oh! the arrogance of modern man.

Scientists across the globe agree that chicken soup really *is* good for cold and flu sufferers. As it simmers, the chicken releases into the broth an amino acid called cysteine which, just like the drug acetylcysteine prescribed for bronchitis and other respiratory ailments, reduces the build up of mucus and helps the patient breathe easier.

Comes as a surprise, doesn't it?

Of course, there is more to old wives' tales than recipes from the Old Country. Old wives' tales are a mixed bag of sayings, folk customs, superstitions, and assertions that pass as common knowledge. Some old wives' tales are ancient, stretching back to biblical times. In St. Matthew's gospel, for example, Jesus paraphrases the old saw, "Red sky at morning, sailors take warning. Red sky at night, sailor's delight." Other old wives' tales are actually new wives' tales: Exhibit A is the belief common among contemporary college students that they can not get pregnant or catch a sexually transmitted disease if they have sex in a hot tub. By the way, the college students are wrong. Very, very wrong.

The sex-in-a-hot-tub fable may be a new wives' tale, but it is perfectly in sync with the old wives' tale tradition. The bulk of old wives' tales concern themselves with the most important events in human life: marriage, sexual relations, pregnancy, childbirth, and raising healthy children. The point of these old wives' tales is to avoid whatever is bad or harmful, attract or encourage whatever is good, and maybe give yourself a bit of an edge by being able to predict what is coming.

Luck is another major preoccupation of old wives. Walking under a ladder invites bad luck. Not killing a ladybug invites good luck. But is there anything to these old folk beliefs? In many cases, the answer is yes. Walking under a ladder is not only unlucky, it can be fatal. Studies in the United States, the United Kingdom, and Sweden have found a near-epidemic of ladder-related accidents. As with stepping around ladders, leaving a ladybug unmolested is also sound advice. They are a gardener's best friends. Ladybugs eat insects that attack tomatoes, cabbages, and broccoli.

Not all good luck/bad luck old wives' tales are rooted in basic safety precautions and rural wisdom. The unluckiness of Friday the 13th, for example, is based on two phobias: fear of Friday and fear of the number 13. It sounds laughable until you discover that every Friday the 13th, between $800 and $900 million in business is lost because people will not board airplanes, or make a major business decision, or dine out at a restaurant, or even show up for work.

One area in which the old wives drop the ball is weather. Since almost all old wives' tales date back to the centuries when the world was more rural than urban, more agricultural than industrial, you would think their observations about the workings of nature would be pretty reliable. But no. The old wives assure us that lightning never strikes the same place twice (tell that to the building manager of the Eiffel Tower). They say that tornadoes can't cross rivers (wrong again!). And their faith in a groundhog's ability to predict the coming of spring is touching, but nonetheless misguided.

In writing this book, I found that collecting old wives' tales was simple. Sorting out whether they were true or not took a lot more legwork. Fortunately for contemporary researchers there is Lexis/Nexis. This godsend of all Internet search engines put at my fingertips a host of articles from medical and scientific journals, as well as food, health and science columns from newspapers around the globe. There are also some excellent books that, whether the authors intended to or not, tackle popular old wives' tales. Among my favorites were Rebecca Rupp's *Weather!*; Michael Shermer's *Why People Believe Weird Things: Pseudoscience, Superstition, And Other Confusions Of Our Time*; *Why Moths Hate Thomas Edison and Other Urgent Inquiries into the Odd Nature of Nature*, edited by Hampton Sides of *Outside* magazine; and *Sex in America: A Definitive Survey* by Robert T. Michael et al.

The question for each old wives' tale is, "How true is it?" You'll find the short answer at the beginning of each tale, with a Veracity Meter designed exclusively for this book by the last twelve winners of the Nobel Prize for Physics, who were themselves assisted by the most senior professors at the Massachusetts Institute of Technology. The result of this unprecedented and painstaking research is a scientifically precise measurement of the reliability of each old wives' tale.

You believe us, right?

Inflated claims of rigorous scientific inquiry notwithstanding, a surprising number of old wives' tales are true—or at least true in part. So dive in, and see for yourself how many of those old superstitions your grandmother passed along to you actually stand up to scientific scrutiny.

Section One

A Dog's Mouth Is Cleaner Than a Human's, and Other Old Wives' Tales to Keep You Healthy

Bacteria Research Results

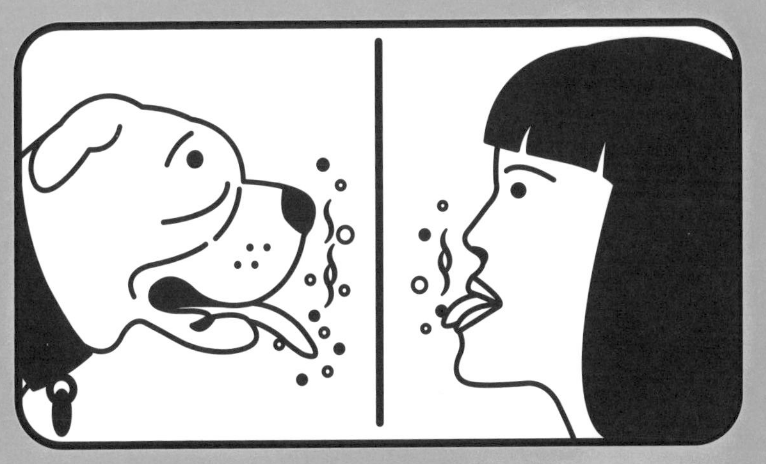

Canine Mouth:
53 types of bacteria

Human Mouth:
37 types of bacteria

A DOG'S MOUTH IS CLEANER THAN A HUMAN'S

How True Is It?
Think twice before giving Spot a kiss.

Get a group of kids playing together and sooner or later one is going to fall and scrape a knee. If the one with the boo-boo is like most kids, he'll look around for a friendly dog to come over and lick the scrape. Why? It's a matter of faith among most kids (and plenty of adults) that a dog's mouth is so clean that a couple of licks from a pooch is as good as a few swabs of antiseptic.

Alas, the dog's-mouth-is-sterile myth is, indeed, a myth.

Dr. Gary "Ask the Vet" Clemons says that "a dog's mouth contains a lot of bacteria." To emphasize his point, Dr. Clemons adds, "Remember, a dog's tongue is not only his washcloth but also his toilet paper."

Researchers at Stanford University found that on average the human mouth harbors 37 types of bacteria. Meanwhile, at the University of Southern California, researchers found that a dog's mouth contains on average 53 types of bacteria.

The sterile dog's mouth Old Wives' Tale goes hand-in-hand with another Old Wives' Tale: that being bitten by a human is more dangerous, in terms of infection and other medical complications, than being bitten by some other animal. It sounds impressive, but the medical literature doesn't back it up. A 1988 study published in the *Annals of Emergency Medicine* found, "Human bites ... do not seem to have any higher risk than animal bites, which have an infection rate of about 10%." The danger rate of human bites only goes up if the wound is left untreated.

The Not-So-Sterile Boxer

A 1996 article in the British medical journal *The Lancet* reported that a 31-year-old British man developed a painful mouth and throat infection known as Ludwig's angina after romping with a friend's boxer dog. Researchers at the Royal Hampshire County Hospital in Winchester, England, where the man was treated, concluded that the dog passed along the infection while licking the man's face.

Analysis of the man's blood revealed the presence of *Pasteurella multocida*, a bacteria found in the mouths of animals and birds. A saliva sample taken from the dog's mouth also was infected with the *Pasteurella multocida* bacteria.

The man recovered after being treated with penicillin.

As for dog bites, the Centers for Disease Control and Prevention reports that in the United States approximately 5 million humans are bitten by dogs every year, with emergency rooms seeing about 1000 dog bite victims per day. And the number of dog bites is growing by leaps and bounds. Over a 10-year period in the United States, the number of dog bites increased by 37%—this in spite of the fact that dog ownership increased by only 2%.

On average in the U.S.A. there are 17 dog-attack fatalities per year. Who are these dogs biting? Not burglars—that's another myth. The chances that your watchdog or house pet will attack and kill a burglar are very low—one in 177. There is a 70% chance, however, that the dog's victim will be a child. According to the *Journal of the American Medical Association*, 333,687 kids visit emergency rooms annually with dog bite injuries, second only to baseball or softball injuries.

And all those dog bites are expensive. In 1995 the insurance industry paid out $250 million in dog bite-related claims. By 2002 that number had jumped to $345.2 million.

Besides, folks who insist that a dog's mouth is sterile are forgetting that by biting, dogs transmit rabies, tetanus, *Pasteurella*, and heaven knows what other nasty and potentially lethal diseases.

You might want to bear that in mind the next time your dog jumps up to lick your face.

IT'S UNHEALTHY TO HOLD BACK A SNEEZE

How True Is It?
Let that sneeze rip!

Just by breathing, you inhale all kinds of dirt, dust, pollen, and other types of microscopic rubbish that float in the air. To clear this nastiness out of your nasal passages, nature developed the sneeze—and not just for humans. Mammals, birds, even reptiles rely on the sneeze for a little sinus housekeeping.

We can't speak for the velocity of a parakeet's sneeze, but when a human sneezes, the microscopic dust flies at more than 100 feet per second. According to Hampton Sides, editor of *Outside* magazine's "The Wild File" column, the force of a human sneeze is on par with the force of a fire hose.

Trying to suppress a sneeze, then, is good manners run amuck. You feel a sneeze coming on because your body has decided that it has reached its quotient of airborne gunk and the time to expel it is now. Besides, suppressing a sneeze truly can be very dangerous.

Sides reports that an unreleased sneeze has been known to cause "fractures in the nasal cartilage, major nosebleeds, burst eardrums, broken blood vessels in the eye, detached retinas, even fatal strokes." Sides goes on to say that if you happen to be ill when trying to clamp down on a sneeze, you could "drive millions of tiny pathogenic particles deep into the sinus tissues, which can lead to serious infections." But there is more. "Alternatively," Sides continues, "it can force air under the skin, causing a condition known as facial emphysema."

So for heaven's sake, the next time you feel a sneeze coming on, just let her rip!

What Happens When We Sneeze?

Lots of things can set off a sneeze. Dust. Pollen. Cat or dog dander. Germs. Pepper. When you breathe in such gunk, the tiny hairs inside your nostrils trap it to keep it from being inhaled into your lungs. As these tiny particles tickle or irritate the inside of your nostrils, your nose transmits a message to what we might call "the sneeze center" of your brain to prepare to expel the unwanted irritant. At that point, the brain sends messages to the various muscle groups that must all work together to generate a sneeze.

The muscles of the abdomen, the chest, the diaphragm, the vocal chords, and the back of the throat all come into play when you sneeze. And there is one other group of muscles at work: the muscles of the eyelids. Every time you sneeze, your eyes close.

LISTENING TO LOUD MUSIC CAUSES DEAFNESS

How True Is It?
This one has a resounding ring of truth.

One of the casualties of rock'n'roll is Pete Townsend: all those years spent playing guitar for The Who in front of massive blaring speakers damaged his auditory nerve. Townsend suffers from tinnitus, hearing loss that is often accompanied by a ringing or buzzing sound in the ears. The damage is permanent: there is no cure for tinnitus.

The sad story of Townsend, combined with a host of anecdotal evidence of club kids who report ringing in the ears even two days after they've been to a club or a rave, reinforces what old wives have been telling us for years: turn down the music or you'll go deaf.

All sound travels through the air as vibrations. These vibrations travel down the ear canal, through the eardrum, into the middle ear and finally into the cochlea, in the inner ear, where the vibrations are registered as sounds. Lining the inner ear are tiny, sensitive hairs. When they encounter vibrations, they shimmy like a 14-year-old girl at a Justin Timberlake concert. Mind-numbingly loud noises at a high frequency can damage or even kill these tiny hairs and lead to hearing loss. What is especially scary is that no pain accompanies hearing loss, so there is no warning signal from the your body that you're in trouble.

A University of Florida study found that hearing loss is on the rise among young people. According to the university's researchers, 17 percent of 10-to-24-year-olds have already lost part of their hearing. The human ear can put up with long

How Long You Can Hear Noises Before It Starts to Become a Problem

The Sight & Hearing Association of the United States Occupational Safety and Health Administration has worked up this list of noises, their decibel levels, and how long you can put up with them—without some type of ear protection—before they endanger your hearing.

Traffic noise, lawn mower	90 decibels	8 hrs.
Motorcycle, power	95 decibels	4 hrs.
Chain saw, train horn	100 decibels	2 hrs.
Helicopter, jackhammer	105 decibels	1 hr.
Snowmobile from the back	110 decibels	30 mins.
Jet skis, crying baby	115 decibels	15 mins.
Rock concert, sand blasting	120 decibels	less than 15 mins.

periods of noise in the 80-to-90 decibel range without being damaged. Yet people who work on road construction, where the noise level is in the generally acceptable 80-to-90 decibel range, wisely protect their ears with ear plugs. Anything above that, however, and all bets are off. The squeal of a subway, for example, measures at 96 decibels. That's not a cause for worry for most mass transit riders, says Janet Mackay, an audiologist at Montreal's Royal Victoria Hospital. But if while riding the subway the commuter is listening to a Walkman—which can play music at 110 decibels—then the risk of hearing trouble increases. So just imagine what happens at a club where the decibel level usually exceeds 120.

So listen to your mother: turn down that noise!

BABIES WHO SUCK THEIR THUMBS WILL HAVE BUCK TEETH

How True Is It?
Truth from the mouths of babes.

Sucking on a thumb or a couple of fingers is hardwired into human babies. Sonograms have shown unborn infants sucking their thumbs. Once a baby comes into the world, sucking at his mother's breast or sucking a bottle becomes associated with warmth and security and the pleasant sensation of the stomach being full. So in situations that make a little child nervous or uncomfortable, sucking on something can be reassuring.

By the way, such oral habits often survive into adulthood as smoking, chewing gum, and snacking.

Among toddlers ages 1 to 3, about 40 percent suck their thumb or fingers. About 33 percent of 3- to 5-year-olds continue to suck their thumbs. And at age 5 the number drops to approximately 25 percent. Thumb-sucking usually disappears in kindergarten or first grade, largely because of peer pressure from the other little darlings in the classroom.

Now that we know that sucking a thumb is natural, normal, and eventually stops, the question remains, "Will it distort the shape of a child's mouth, create buck teeth, or otherwise require a small fortune in orthodontic work years later?" The answer is a qualified yes. According to the American Academy of Pediatric Dentistry, long-term sucking on a finger, pacifier, or some other object can push the upper front teeth outward or otherwise distort the position of the teeth.

A pacifier may be a solution for a small child who sucks his thumb. These are soft and designed not to put pressure on the mouth. Nonetheless, there is no guarantee that using a pacifier now will fend off dental trouble later. All that said, Jane Brody, health editor of the *New York Times*, assures parents that in most cases, "as long as the habit is relinquished before the permanent teeth begin to emerge at about age 6, it rarely has a significant influence on mouth structures or tooth positions."

READING IN DIM LIGHT WILL RUIN YOUR EYES

How True Is It?
This tale is none too bright.

Turning the lights down low may create atmosphere, but it drives old wives to distraction. "Turn on more lights!" they cry. "Do you want to go blind?"

And at first, you might think that the old wives are right. Trying to read in dim light strains the eyes. Eyestrain could lead to eye damage. Read in the semi-dark often enough, and perhaps you will eventually go blind. Such step-by-step reasoning seems unassailable, but before you fire up every lamp in the house, let's ask an expert.

Dr. Eugene Folk is quoted in *Eye Facts*, a publication of the Eye Center of the University of Illinois at Chicago College of Medicine, as saying, "Although reading in dim light is unwise because it may cause your eyes to feel tired or uncomfortable, it can't hurt your eyes." You can hear the old wives revving up to raise the issue of reading small print, but Dr. Folk is one step ahead of them. "Similarly, reading small print or reading extensively cannot cause damage to the eyes," he says. "This is true even for people who already have poor vision."

The American Academy of Ophthalmology (AAO) backs up everything Dr. Folk said. "You can't wear out your eyes by using them," says the AAO, even if you use them in poor lighted situations. The only issue in regard to reading in dim light is "good light makes reading easier and prevents eye fatigue."

But what about spending hours working on a computer? Surely that must cause eye damage. Once again, the AAO is reassuring. "Working on computers will not harm your eyes. However, you can develop eyestrain or fatigue after working at a terminal for long periods of time, just as you can from reading and other close work." The AAO recommends that you take regular breaks from the computer. If you can't leave your work often during the day, then just looking away from the screen at an object across the room will help.

MORE PEOPLE COMMIT SUICIDE BETWEEN CHRISTMAS AND NEW YEAR'S THAN AT ANY OTHER TIME OF THE YEAR

How True Is It?
You might as well believe that reindeer can fly.

It is an article of faith among contemporary old wives that the stress, anxiety, and loneliness of the holidays drive droves of unhappy individuals to suicide. But Dr. Herbert Hendin, medical director of the American Foundation for Suicide Prevention, says it just ain't so. He told a *New York Daily News* reporter, "I'd get calls every season from people who wanted to do a story on suicide and the holidays, and when I told them it wasn't true, they would get depressed!"

The National Center for Health Statistics confirms Dr. Hendin's claims. After studying the NCHS's cause-of-death data over a period of years Dr. Hendin found that December is actually the lowest month of the year for suicides. January is pretty close to the bottom, too. Many psychiatrists believe the rate is so low at Christmas because it is a season when people tend to be more in touch with each other than at any other time of the year.

So what season does see the highest suicide rate? Surprisingly, spring and summer. Why would more people take their lives when the weather is beautiful and all of nature is burgeoning? The experts don't have an answer. Yet. But they have recognized the pattern, which explains why April is National Suicide Prevention Month.

Singapore's *The Straits Times* reports that in this nation-city that has no seasons, people tend to commit suicide on prominent holidays. Of the 300 to 400 suicides recorded in Singapore annually,

Another Urban Legend

Dr. Harvey Roy Greenberg, a Manhattan psychiatrist and author of *Emotional Illness in the Family*, calls the Christmas suicide thing "a psychiatric urban myth." In this respect it is like other holiday myths—for example, the widespread phobia that at Halloween our neighbors transform into ghouls who slip razor blades into apples and sprinkle cyanide on candy. Alan Dundes, a professor of folklore at the University of California at Berkeley, says that the Halloween phobia is baseless, too, and urges people who don't believe him to check the police blotters.

most occur on the second day of Chinese New Year, New Year's Day, Christmas, Labour Day, or the Hindu holiday Deepavali. Statistics in Singapore have found that holiday-related depression is not why people take their lives. Financial trouble is the leading cause for suicide among Singapore men—about 33 percent killed themselves because they had lost money on an investment, through gambling, had fallen deeply into debt, or were being pressured by loan sharks.

According to *The Guardian* (London), Dr. Jan Birtle, a psychotherapist and lecturer in psychiatry at Birmingham University, has found that men are twice as likely to kill themselves as women. But attempted suicide is much more common among women—especially in the under-35 age group—than among men. Most often women place the blame for their attempted suicide on relationship problems. Which brings us to a depressing statistic: In Birmingham, England, three casualty departments (known as emergency rooms in the United States) reported 69 women who had attempted suicide on Valentine's Day. This contrasts with less than 30 attempted suicides on two "neutral," or non-holiday, days selected from the calendar.

TOADS GIVE YOU WARTS

How True Is It?
Kissing one is just as likely to turn it into a prince as give you warts.

The skin glands of toads secrete a slimy substance that can raise your blood pressure, give you hallucinations, and in some cases poison any dog or cat dumb enough to try to eat it. The skin of the cane toad, for example, is slick with a toxic compound called bufotenine. In Australia, scientists have found dead snakes that were killed so quickly by bufotenine that the cane toad the snake tried to eat was still in the snake's mouth, unswallowed. Some tribes in South America dip darts and arrows in cane-toad toxin to kill their prey, and lick the secretion right off the cane toads to achieve a hallucinogenic ecstasy during religious ceremonies.

But neither the toad's toxic gunk, nor the toad as a whole, will give you warts.

Warts are caused by papillomaviruses, a family of more than 70 viruses that afflict primates such as apes and humans. Toads and all other amphibians do not get papillomaviruses.

In most cases when a papillomavirus makes contact with your skin, your body's immune system gets rid of it. If your immune system isn't operating very well, then the virus stays and you get warts.

Warts are one of the most common skin conditions on the planet. As you read this, one in every ten persons has at least one wart. And 75 percent of the human population will have at least one wart in his or her lifetime.

Most warts will go away on their own (after a year or so). If you'd rather not wait that long, a doctor can treat your warts with

Warts on Your Sole

Among the most unpleasant warts are plantar warts which develop on the bottom of the feet. Because they are thick and the virus-infected area tends to reach deep into the foot tissue, plantar warts can even make walking awkward and painful. Plantar warts can be removed surgically, but your walk will remain affected until the wound is fully healed. Depending on the size of the wart, healing could take weeks. If the plantar wart is caught early enough, when it is still very small, your doctor can remove it with liquid nitrogen. Once the plantar wart is larger than a centimeter in diameter, however, it's too big for a liquid nitrogen treatment. At that point, surgery is the only option.

liquid nitrogen, which does not require a local anesthesia and eliminates the warts with minimal or no scarring.

Although toads cannot give you warts, raw meat and fish can. People who handle raw poultry, beef, and fish often develop what are known as "butcher's warts." Why working with raw meat or fish should produce warts is one of those mysteries which modern medicine still cannot explain.

IF YOU CROSS YOUR EYES, THEY WILL STAY THAT WAY

How True Is It?
Look askance at this one.

Old wives take particular delight in warning children that an action that appears to be completely innocent will result in dire, lifelong consequences. Crossing your eyes as a means of mindless entertainment is one of them.

Crossed eyes (the doctors call it strabismus) is serious business. But you can not cause it by playing at having it. There is no tiny switch behind your eyeballs waiting to lock into place because you were dumb enough to cross your eyes.

Let's look at the real causes of crossed eyes. In most cases, a kid inherits the condition from his or her parents. Loss of vision in one eye can cause strabismus. So can any of a host of eye diseases. There are also cases in which the eye muscles are fine, but the coordination mechanism for the two eyes doesn't work properly.

Children do not outgrow strabismus, but they can be treated. Eyeglasses will often do the trick—and they have been prescribed, with good results, for babies as young as six months. If one eye turns outward, or if the eyes are not aligned properly (meaning one eye is higher than the other), then surgery is required. And it is the eye muscles that are operated on, not the eyes themselves. In almost all cases, one operation is all it takes to correct the problem.

IF YOU GO OUTSIDE WITH WET HAIR OR WET FEET, YOU'LL CATCH A COLD

How True Is It?
You might catch some strange looks from your neighbors, but not a cold.

The idea that walking around in winter weather with wet feet or wet hair will bring on a cold is one of the most firmly entrenched old wives' tales. For more than 100 years scientists have been methodically debunking this myth, but this is one fable people just won't give up.

One of the world's top experts on the common cold, Dr. Jack M. Gwaltney Jr., an emeritus professor of medicine at the University of Virginia, explains that, "Health and the weather was a big topic in previous periods of history." Scientists have noticed that some infectious diseases follow a seasonal pattern, but they don't understand why.

What scientists do know, however, is that a cold is caused by one of several hundred different strains of viruses that plague the planet. According to the United States National Institutes of Health, every year approximately one billion people worldwide suffer from colds. All these cold sufferers picked up the colds by coming into contact with a cold virus, either by touching something contaminated with cold virus germs, such as a telephone or a stair rail, or being near someone who has a cold and whose sneezing or coughing is spraying cold germs into the air. And that may account for winter being designated "cold and flu season": with more people confined together indoors, it is easier for the cold virus to spread.

After World War II researchers at the Common Cold

Research Unit in Salisbury, England, recruited a dozen volunteers to take a bath, then wander up and down a cold corridor in wet socks and their bathing suits for as long as they could stand it. Their body temperature dropped a few degrees, and they felt pretty miserable, but in the end these damp dozen did not catch more colds than other people in the same building who had been warm and dry.

In the 1950s in Chicago researchers brought in 253 volunteers to see if being cold would indeed produce more colds. One group sat in a 60-degree Fahrenheit room in nothing but their socks and underwear. Another group sat in a freezer, bundled up in warm clothing. Both groups caught colds at exactly the same rate.

Time and again researchers have returned to this question, and each time they have come to the same conclusion: being cold and wet doesn't increase your likelihood of catching a cold, nor will it make the cold you already have worse.

The data is remarkably consistent. If only the researchers could get people to believe it.

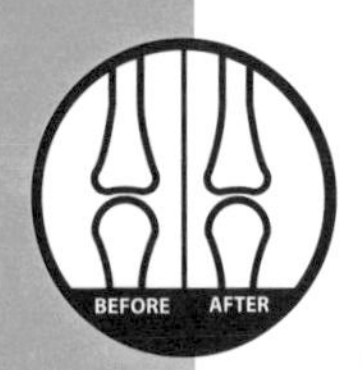

CRACK YOUR KNUCKLES AND YOU'LL DEVELOP ARTHRITIS

How True Is It?
Your knuckles are pretty safe—but you might send shivers down someone's spine.

There's an urban legend among bone specialists about a kid who had been told that if he continued to crack his knuckles he'd get arthritis. In the interests of science, the kid became his own guinea pig. For years he cracked the knuckles of just one of his hands. When he was all grown up and had become a doctor, he X-rayed his hands to see if the knuckle-cracking one showed any susceptibility for arthritis. Not only did he see no sign of incipient arthritis, he found no discernible physical difference between his two hands.

This is folklore nirvana: perhaps the one and only occasion when an old wives' tale is debunked by an urban legend.

Like the boy wonder of the urban legend, medical science has found no link between knuckle-cracking and arthritis. Furthermore, rare individuals who can bend their thumbs back until they touch their wrists are in no more danger than anyone else for arthritis. What these life-of-the-party people do have is ligamentous laxity, which just means that their ligaments enjoy greater flexibility than is the case with most of us. As orthopedic surgeon Dr. Donald Longjohn puts it, "Some people are a little more loose than others."

But even ligamentous laxity has its limits. Folks who can dislocate their shoulders or pop some other joint at will really are asking for trouble. Repeatedly popping a joint in and out of its socket does damage the joint. Once a joint becomes unstable, it is impossible to reverse the problem.

It's possible that the old wives' tale about cracking your knuckles is based on a hunch that repeating a certain action will damage your body. And it is true that there are repetitive tasks that can lead to arthritis. The act of driving large, hard-to-steer, heavy equipment such as a school bus puts everyday pressure on certain joints, and that can lead to arthritis.

But knuckle crackers don't get off scot-free. Two researchers, Jorge Castellanos and David Axelrod, of Toledo, Ohio, published the results of their study of long-term knuckle-cracking in the *Annals of Rheumatic Diseases*. Castellanos and Axelrod found that people over age 45 who were still cracking their knuckles suffered from swollen hands and had lost some of the strength and sureness of their grip. Knuckle-cracking over a long period overstretches, and may even tear, the ligaments in the fingers. This can develop into swelling and loss of hand strength.

Section Two

If You're Carrying the Baby High, It's a Girl, and Other Old Wives' Tales About Pregnancy

IF YOU'RE CARRYING THE BABY HIGH, IT'S A GIRL

How True Is It?
About 50 percent of the time.

The invention of ultrasound took a lot of steam out of the gender-guessing industry. Nonetheless, the old methods of gender divination are still around—probably because they are a lot more fun than a visit to the obstetrician.

Where the mother is carrying her baby is said to be a sure-fire method of determining its gender. If you are carrying high, it's a girl. If you are carrying low, it's a boy. Doctors tell us, however, that the high/low thing is not a sign of the sex of the baby; rather, the shape of the mother's belly is an indication of her uterine and muscle tone combined with the baby's position. For example, the old wives will look at a woman who is carrying her baby low and say, "Ah ha! She's going to have a boy!" In fact, all that has happened is the baby has dropped lower into the pelvis because the mother is getting closer to delivery.

Then there is the basketball vs. watermelon theory. If a pregnant woman looks like she's carrying a perfectly round basketball, it's a boy. If she looks like she's carrying a wide watermelon, it's a girl. Statistically, that myth came out as a dead heat. You might as well toss a coin.

There are, of course, other traditional methods, all equally questionable. Mothers who can't get enough sweets will have a girl. Mothers who crave anything sour will have a boy.

Some people say breast size can reveal the baby's sex. If the mother's right breast is larger, she's having a boy. If her left breast is larger, she's having a girl.

Not Quite 50 Percent of the Time

It is conventional to say that these pregnancy-related old wives' tales have a 50-50 chance of being correct. In fact, the odds are not so even. Globally, for every 100 girls born, between 104 and 107 boys are born. Recently in China the number has become much more skewed: in 2002, for every 100 girls, 116.9 boys were born. The preponderance of boys is an artificially created phenomenon thanks to the Chinese government's policy of one child per family. Many Chinese families prefer that their only child be a boy rather than a girl. A September 1995 article published in Hong Kong's *South China Morning Post* reported it is not uncommon in China for women to abort a female fetus, or abandon a female infant and not report its birth, then try again in hopes of conceiving a boy.

The number of infants girls left at Chinese orphanages is so high that in 2002 Americans adopted 33,637 Chinese baby girls. Population experts predict that if this trend continues, by 2020 there will be 40 million more men than women in China.

A related story published in 2002 in the *South China Morning Post* said that parents with only one little boy are producing a generation of spoiled, undisciplined, "little emperors." Teachers report a wave of behavior problems at school where, perhaps for the first time in their lives, these little boys are hearing the word "No." And sociologists wonder what will happen decades from now when the "little emperors'" parents are elderly and there are no brothers and sisters around to help share the burden.

Another rumored tell-tale sign is the physical condition of the father. If Dad starts putting on weight, his wife will have a girl. If he doesn't gain any weight at all, she's having a boy.

And then there's the original at-home pregnancy test. Take a gold pendant and hang it from a chain. Suspend the chain over the mother's belly. If the chain swings back and forth, it's a boy. If it moves in a circle, it's a girl.

A popular new method in the West is the Chinese Infant Gender Statistic Chart. This method begins by helping a woman compute her Chinese age and identify her conception month according to the Chinese lunar calendar. Once these two numbers have been determined, the chart reveals whether you will have a boy or a girl.

IF A PREGNANT WOMAN'S FACE IS PUFFY, SHE'S GOING TO HAVE A GIRL

How True Is It?
There's a blush of truth to this one.

According to the old wives, an unborn girl saps her mother's good looks—hence the puffy face, straggly hair, and extra weight around the pregnant woman's hips. There may be something to this old wives' tale, but if so, it is not an example of *in utero* family rivalry. Some scientists have speculated that when a woman is carrying a girl, her body produces more estrogen. It is the estrogen that packs more fat on the hips. As for the stringy hair and puffy face, the scientists cannot come to any conclusions.

If science is studying possible links between thin, lifeless hair and the gender of an unborn child, it might as well branch out into other unconventional methods of predicting a baby's sex. Psychologist Janet DiPietro, who studies fetal development at the Johns Hopkins School of Public Health in Baltimore, has conducted a study of the dreams of 104 pregnant mothers, all of whom had more than 12 years of formal schooling. About 75 percent of the time, women who dreamed they would have a boy did indeed give birth to a boy, and women who dreamed they would have a girl gave birth to a girl. Interestingly, the dreams of pregnant women with less schooling were an accurate predictor only 43 percent of the time—which places their dreams solidly in the coin-toss territory.

IF THE LABOR IS DIFFICULT, THE MOTHER IS ABOUT TO GIVE BIRTH TO A BOY

How True Is It?
The old wives may be on to something.

In Ireland, old wives who double as midwives say that a difficult delivery means that a boy is coming. So between 1997 and 2000, researchers conducted a study at the National Maternity Hospital in Dublin, Ireland. They based their study on 4070 boys and 4005 girls born to first-time mothers. The results surprised everyone (except the old wives).

A new mother had a 76 percent chance—or better—of an easy delivery if she was carrying a girl. Her chances dipped to 71 percent if she was carrying a boy. Equipment such as forceps were necessary in the delivery of 23 percent of boy newborns, only 18 percent of girl newborns. Furthermore, 6 percent of the boys delivered required a Caesarean section, while just a shade over 4 percent of the girls required one.

While the study produced intriguing numbers, it has not been able to suggest a cause. There is supporting data that newborn boys have larger heads than newborn girls, which could prolong labor and require Caesarean sections. But baby boys are also more likely to experience fetal distress, which has nothing to do with head size. So, in spite of the Irish study, the reason for the correlation between gender and a difficult delivery remains a mystery.

IF THE BABY IS LATE, THE MOTHER SHOULD TAKE LONG WALKS

How True Is It?
Anyone who'd buy this one should take a hike.

Old wives have tremendous sympathy for pregnant women, hence the large number of pregnancy-related myths. The leaders of this particular pack are two genres of old wives' tales: "How to Tell the Baby's Gender" and "How to Get the Baby to Come Out."

There are women who blithely declare that they have easy pregnancies, that they felt fine during the whole nine months. One prays these insensitive ladies do not make such comments in front of women who suffered months of back, leg, and groin pain from lugging all that extra weight around, are now past their due date, and just want the damn kid to be born already. As you'd expect, the old wives offer remedies that will encourage the unborn child to get the ball rolling.

Expectant mothers are told that taking long walks will induce labor. Dr. Jonathan Schaffir, a clinical assistant professor of obstetrics and gynecology at the Ohio State University Medical Center, found that two out of three pregnant women believed walking brings on labor. In December 2000 he interviewed 102 pregnant women from the region around Columbus, Ohio, asking their opinions of ten common recommendations on how to get the baby to come. Of those 102 expectant moms, 84 percent had heard that walking worked, and 64 percent believed it was true.

Those women were indulging in a little wishful thinking. Walking does not induce labor. In fact, the staff of the Mayo

Clinic has stated bluntly, "No one knows for sure what triggers labor—and every woman's experience is unique." All that can be said for certain is that there are typical symptoms that tell a woman her body is getting ready to go into labor. These signs include the baby settling deeper into the mother's pelvis, the softening, thinning, or dilation of the cervix, even a sudden burst of energetic housekeeping known as "nesting."

Another common old wives' tale is that having sex will bring the baby. This one is regarded with such certainty that it has a corollary old wives' tale: if the mother has sex early in her pregnancy she runs the risk of miscarriage or premature delivery. A study published by the American College of Obstetrics and Gynecology found that having sex does *not* increase miscarriages, premature deliveries, or hasten the delivery of the full-term child.

Some old wives encourage mothers to eat spicy food to jumpstart childbirth. More often than not, the following day the mother has heartburn, not a new baby.

Castor oil is another popular folk remedy to move nature along. And here the old wives may have been on to something. Castor oil can cause contractions, but researchers have found that it can cause such severe contractions as to harm the unborn child.

What does Dr. Schaffir recommend? "For healthy pregnancies, Mother Nature is the best obstetrician," he says. "These things take time."

IF YOU CRAVE SPICY FOOD, YOU'RE HAVING A BOY; IF YOU CRAVE SWEET FOOD, IT'S A GIRL

How True Is It?
There could be a grain of truth to this food fable.

According to the old wives, if a pregnant woman has a yen for Szechuan food, she should start thinking of boys' names. But if she can't stay away from the chocolatier, then a girl is on the way.

We have to admit that there is no evidence to support the spicy-or-sweet connection. But there has been one interesting study that finds a link between what an expectant mother eats and the sex of her unborn child.

Professor Dimitrios Trichopoulos of Harvard University's School of Public Health followed the pregnancies of 250 American women. He found that women who gave birth to boys ate 8 percent more protein, 9 percent more carbohydrates, 11 percent more animal fats, and 15 percent more vegetable fats than women who gave birth to girls. Professor Trichopoulos proposes that a woman's body may be receiving signals from her unborn son, generated by the testosterone secreted from the fetal testicles, to eat more. The professor suggests that this could explain why newborn boys tend to weigh 100 grams more than newborn girls. Professor Trichopoulos hasn't insisted that his study is conclusive and irrefutable, but it is interesting.

Of course, there will always be scoffers. Elisabeth Gasparini, dietitian at Melbourne, Australia's Royal Women's Hospital, insists that the only way to find out the sex of an unborn baby is via ultrasound. And while she was in debunking mode, Gasparini also took a swipe at another food-based old wives' tale: that a pregnant mother should increase her food intake because she is eating for two. "Energy requirements for mothers-to-be are only slightly higher than normal," Gasparini says, "and it's the quality of the food that's important, not the quantity."

What to Eat When You're Pregnant

- Milk, yogurt, hard pasteurized cheese such as cheddar, and fish such as salmon for calcium that will strengthen the baby's bones. But be careful! Do not eat unpasteurized blue cheeses or pasteurized soft cheeses while pregnant. These can carry a bacterium called *Listeria monocytogenes*, which can cause miscarriage.
- Red meat, legumes, nuts, whole-grain cereals and green leafy vegetables for a healthy amount of iron in the infant's blood.
- Citrus fruits, berries, tomatoes, cabbage, broccoli and cauliflower for Vitamin C to encourage the development of healthy teeth, gums, bones, and tissue.

VOLUPTUOUS WOMEN WERE BUILT FOR CHILD-BEARING

How True Is It?
Mother Nature knew what she was doing.

Throughout human history old wives have assured curvaceous women, "You have the hips for child-bearing." It's meant as a compliment. Although these days, when undernourished actresses and pop stars have the look women are supposed to want, it's not likely to win an old wife any friends.

A 2004 article in Melbourne, Australia's *Herald Sun* reported that scientists in the United States have found that shapely women really are designed by nature to make babies. Women with large hips, a narrow waist, and a big bust were found to have more fertility hormones than reed-thin women.

The data was based on a study of 119 women. Over a period of several months the researchers collected daily saliva samples from the women and recorded the levels of oestradiol and progesterone, two hormones that are essential to fertility. At the women's most fertile times of the month, the fertility hormone level of large-hipped women was 37 percent higher than that of their slender sisters.

The big-hip syndrome also has reverberations among men. Who are the classic sex goddesses? Marilyn Monroe. Sophia Loren. Mae West. Jayne Mansfield. And these days, Jennifer Lopez. All bodacious, voluptuous females who fit perfectly the requirements of this latest study. Why are they the fantasy objects of so many millions of men? The researchers suggest that it's a subconscious thing that has evolved over thousands of years: trial and error has taught countless generations of men to be drawn to women who are most likely to reproduce. In other words, women with the hips for child-bearing.

Section Three

Lightning Never Strikes the Same Place Twice, and Other Old Wives' Tales About the Weather

LIGHTNING NEVER STRIKES THE SAME PLACE TWICE

How True Is It?
Way off the mark.

A small mountain of data tells us that lightning does in fact strike the same spot more than once. Some places are actually lightning magnets. Two of the world's most famous lightning rods are Paris' Eiffel Tower and New York City's Empire State Building: on average, both are struck by lightning 25 to 30 times every year. The Petronas Towers in Kuala Lumpur, Malaysia, and the Sears Tower in Chicago attract their share of electrical excitement, too.

One spectacular example of lightning striking the same place more than once, and in rapid succession, occurred among the tight cluster of skyscrapers that form the heart of downtown Oklahoma City, Oklahoma. These high-rise towers have been a favorite target for lightning bolts from the moment they were built. In one of Mother Nature's more dramatic demonstrations of just how offbase an old wives' tale can be, on May 29, 2001, these towers were struck repeatedly every 10 to 30 seconds.

And buildings aren't the only thing that can attract lightning more than once. According to *The Guinness Book of World Records*, Roy Sullivan of Virginia holds the record for a human being who has suffered the most lightning strikes: between 1942 and 1977 he was hit seven times.

Lightning Facts

- A typical lightning bolt is about one inch wide.
- On average, a lightning bolt burns at about 27,000° Fahrenheit (14,982.2° Celsius). That's hotter than the surface of the sun (9,000 degrees Fahrenheit).
- A lightning bolt generates 10-30 million volts of electricity (a New York City subway train runs on 600 volts of electricity).
- Lightning cranks out 25-30 thousand amps of electrical current (a household outlet produces about 15 amps).
- On average, every commercial airliner in regular use takes two lightning strikes every year.
- Each second, between 50 and 100 lightning bolts strike the Earth.
- Lightning strikes most often in Central Africa, Florida, and Asia's Himalayas mountain range.
- It strikes least often in the Pacific islands, the North Pole, and the South Pole.

NO TWO SNOWFLAKES ARE EXACTLY ALIKE

How True Is It?
This one's no joke.

How could it be that no two snowflakes would ever be alike, that every single individual snowflake would be one of a kind? In his explanation, Kenneth G. Libbrecht of Caltech starts with electrons. According to Professor Libbrecht, particle physics tells us that because electrons have no component parts—in other words, they aren't made up of other things—one electron looks exactly like every other electron.

A snowflake, or snow crystal, as Libbrecht calls them, is made up of about 10 quintillion water molecules (a quintillion is a 1 followed by 18 zeros). In order for two snow crystals to be exactly alike, all those water molecules would have to arrange themselves in precisely the same positions. But they don't, and not just because there are 10 quintillion parts to deal with. As the water molecules float from the clouds through the sky toward the ground, they are affected by changes in the temperature, the amount of moisture in the air, and collisions with the microscopic bits of ash and dust that fill Earth's atmosphere. As the snow crystal makes it way through this obstacle course, it assumes a random, complex, and very beautiful pattern. Given the 10 quintillion water molecules and the unpredictable impediments the snow crystal encounters, Libbrecht assures us, "the probability of two crystals growing with exactly the same pattern of dislocations is vanishingly small." Libbrecht does leave a little wiggle room for the extremely remote possibility that somehow all the random elements that create a snowflake could somehow be repeated. But by his calculations, "the odds of it happening within the lifetime of the universe are essentially zero."

IF A GROUNDHOG SEES ITS SHADOW ON FEBRUARY 2, WE'LL HAVE SIX MORE WEEKS OF WINTER

How True Is It?
It depends on which groundhog you're watching.

Thanks to the 1993 romantic comedy *Groundhog Day*, starring Bill Murray and Andie McDowell, many of us are familiar with Punxsutawney, Pennsylvania. At least since 1887, this little town has been relying on its famous groundhog, Phil, to predict if winter is over or if we're in for another six weeks of nasty weather.

It's all very scientific, of course. On February 2, just about halfway between the winter solstice and the spring equinox, all eyes turn to a groundhog burrow. If the groundhog comes out and sees his shadow, he gets frightened, scampers back inside, and winter drags on for another six weeks. If the groundhog does not see his shadow, however, then he goes off on his merry way and we can look forward to an early spring.

The people of Punxsutawney insist that their groundhog, Punxsutawney Phil, is the one and only entirely reliable prognosticator of the coming of spring. Certainly the movie has gone a long way to making Punxsutawney Phil the world's most famous groundhog. It has transformed the town's celebration of Groundhog Day from a modest local event into a major celebration with crowds of visitors cramming into Punxsutawney to witness Phil's remarkable feat of forecasting.

The Punxsutawneyians claim that Phil's predictions are 100% accurate. A quick look at the numbers, however, makes one wonder if perhaps Phil's stats haven't been massaged by Punxsutawney's Visitors and Conventions Bureau. In fact, Phil's accuracy rate hovers at or below the 39 percent mark. If Vegas were giving Groundhog Day odds, the smart money would not be on Phil.

It may be heresy—or at least treason—but other localities tout their own groundhogs. Shubenacadie Sam, who makes his home in Nova Scotia's Shubenacadie Wildlife Park, claims to be Canada's first prognosticating groundhog. In 1979, on what must have been a slow day for legislation, the Ohio General Assembly declared Buckeye Chuck of Marion, Ohio, the official State Groundhog. Meanwhile in Louisiana, where nothing is what you would expect it to be, the state groundhog is actually a crawfish named Claude.

Giving Phil a serious run for his money is New York City's Staten Island Chuck, who has rendered predictions that Staten Islanders insist are 84 percent accurate!

Chuck's handlers would also like to offer you the Brooklyn Bridge at a very reasonable price.

PEOPLE AND ANIMALS BEHAVE STRANGELY DURING A FULL MOON

How True Is It?
This one might be full of it.

The terms "loony" and "lunatic" both come from the Latin word *luna*, which means, "the moon." As old wives' tales go, belief in the link between odd ball behavior and a full moon is extremely ancient. And the anecdotal evidence to back up the old wives is extensive.

In 2000, doctors at England's Bradford Royal Infirmary reported that during the three days on and around the full moon, they treated twice as many patients for animal bites, which suggested to them that the moon might be getting the animals worked up. In terms of human mayhem, a 1987 survey reported that 80 percent of emergency room nurses and 64 percent of emergency room doctors believed they saw more murder victims during a full moon than on other days of the month.

The anecdotal evidence doesn't end there. The notorious 1970s New York City serial killer, David Berkowitz ("Son of Sam") killed five of his eight victims during a full moon. Serial killer Charles Hyde, who terrified England in the 1880s, did most of his murdering under a full moon. (By the way, the Hyde case was the inspiration for Robert Louis Stevenson's novel, *Dr. Jekyll and Mr. Hyde*).

Meanwhile, the *British Medical Journal* found links between the full moon and a sharp increase in criminal behavior, as well as drunkenness, drug overdoses, and even traffic accidents.

In 2002 *The San Francisco Chronicle* conducted its own study to see if there was any link between a full moon and the number of murders committed in the city between 1997 and 2001. The reporters found that in 1997 there were nine full-moon murders; seven in 1998; seven in 1999; nine in 2000; and 14 in 2001. On the surface, the numbers look impressive—until you realize that the reporters failed to compare the number of murders on nights with a full moon murders against the number of murders committed on nights when the moon was not full.

Alas, sloppy studies only reinforce the full-moon myth. Another example: in the 1970s University of Miami psychologist Arthur Lieber surveyed 15 years of data from the Dade County police department's homicide files and concluded that murders followed the phases of the moon, with the number of homicides reaching their peak at the full moon. But Lieber's "data" didn't stand up under examination. An astronomer, Nicholas Sanduleak, double-checked Lieber's figures and found no correlation between the full moon and an increase in homicides. It didn't help Lieber's case that, to account for the rise and fall of homicides, he offered the novel and decidedly unscientific suggestion that because the human body is mostly water and the moon has influence on the tides, the pull of a full moon affects people in unpredictable ways.

San Francisco's coroner, Dr. Boyd Stephens, has a different theory. A night with a full moon is attractive and exciting. On such a night, Dr. Stephens says, "People tend to go outdoors, they tend to drink, they tend to party, and that's when they get in trouble."

It appears, then, that in the case of the truth or falsehood of this old wives' tale, the jury is still out—but the anecdotal evidence urges caution.

A RED SKY IN THE MORNING MEANS A STORM IS COMING

How True Is It?
Seafaring folklore worth heeding.

Even people who've never owned a boat know the adage, "Red sky at morning, sailors take warning. Red sky at night, sailor's delight." But the proverb is not limited to sailors. In St. Matthew's gospel Christ says, "When it is evening, you say, 'It will be fair weather for the sky is red.' And in the morning, 'Today there will be a storm, for the sky is red and lowering'" (Matthew 16, 2-3). Which leads us to believe that not just seafarers but everyone from shepherds in the hills of Bethlehem to fishermen on the Sea of Galilee were familiar with this bit of weather folklore.

At the risk of sounding like Doubting Thomas, we'd still like some data before we accept that the maxim is true.

And it is! According to Joe Sienkiewicz, chief of the Ocean Applications Branch and a science and operations officer with the NOAA/NWS Ocean Prediction Center, the saying applies to Earth's mid-latitudes where weather systems—clear or stormy—move from west to east. When the morning sun rises on an approaching storm, it casts its light on "the approaching mid- and high-level clouds to create a red sky in the morning."

On the other hand, Sienkiewicz explains, if the sun sets in the evening "as a weather system exits and high pressure is building, then the departing clouds would be illuminated. This would create a red sky at night with fair weather to follow."

So the saying is true, as long as the weather is moving in its usual west-to-east pattern. Once in a great while, however, a weather system will travel from south to north, and in that case, the "red sky" old wives' tale does not apply.

How True Are Those Weather Proverbs?

In 1954, R.E. Spencer, formerly of the National Weather Service in the United States, published an article in "Weekly Weather and Crop Bulletin" on the reliability of weather forecasting proverbs, and a few disparities. For example:

- "The south wind is the father of the poor." Not in the southern states of the USA! Spencer observed that along the Gulf of Mexico and the Atlantic Ocean the south wind is "the wettest, stormiest, and generally least pleasant of winds."
- " A western wind carrieth water in his hand." This one does pan out if you live on the western slope of the Sierra, Nevada or Cascade mountains where the western wind does bring rain or snow. If you live on the eastern slopes of these mountains, however, it is the eastern winds that bring moisture.

It makes one wonder: if such weather folklore is so far off base, why have these proverbs endured for so many generations? "The trouble with weather proverbs," Spencer wrote, "is not so much that they're all wrong, but that they're not all right for all times in all places." According to Spencer, most weather proverbs prove to be false because their place of origin is the Mediterranean, or Scandinavia, or the Middle East, and do not apply to other places where weather conditions are dramatically different.

ARTHRITIS FLARES UP IN WET WEATHER

How True Is It?
The only thing that flares up in wet weather is your perm.

Arthritis sufferers will tell you that their pains flare up when the weather turns damp. But Donald A. Redelmeier, a professor of medicine at the University of Toronto, says it's unlikely that dampness would have any effect on arthritis. In the first place, Dr. Redelmeier says, the "skin surrounding joints is rather impervious to water and most people stay dry indoors during rain anyway. In addition, arthritis patients do not experience dramatic changes in their symptoms when immersed in water (such as during baths or swimming)."

Perhaps it's the drop in barometric pressure that causes the flareups. But Dr. Redelmeier finds that arthritis sufferers do not complain of increased pain during a plane flight or while driving a car through the mountains—two situations in which the body experiences greater swings in barometric pressure than when it rains.

Then maybe it's the humidity that's the culprit? Dr. Redelmeier doesn't buy that theory, either. "Hospitalized patients are often given humidified air to breathe," he says, "and this has little apparent effect on arthritis conditions." And he goes on to point out that taking a nice long shower will certainly fill the bathroom with humidity—yet arthritis patients don't regard showers as something to be avoided.

Dr. Redelmeier concedes that he would not describe any of the arthritis/wet weather studies as flawless, but slight glitches in the data would not account for the widespread and deeply rooted belief that dampness makes arthritis worse.

The solution probably lies in the realm of psychology, a field which has known for years that "people often see patterns even where none exist." Dr. Redelmeier reminds us that arthritis pain increasing on a wet day is a random event. Someone with arthritis probably gets through a host of damp, dreary days without feeling a twinge. But all it takes is one major, unforgettable flareup on a stormy day and the arthritis sufferer will "pay more attention to confirming evidence, neglect contrary evidence, and misinterpret ambiguous evidence, thereby entrenching the belief."

It appears, then, that the link between arthritis and the weather is more in the head than in the joints.

IT CAN BE TOO COLD TO SNOW

How True Is It?
It's the cold, hard truth.

At first glance, the old saying, "It's too cold to snow," seems idiotic. It would be like saying that your freezer is too cold to make ice. Come on, the only time it snows is when it's cold, right?

Actually, no. In this case the old wives who specialize in weather folklore know what they are talking about. Matt Peroutka, a meteorologist at the National Weather Service's Techniques Development Laboratory in Silver Spring, Maryland, explains, "The atmosphere must contain moisture to generate snow, and very cold air contains very little moisture. Once the air temperature at ground level drops below about -10 degrees Fahrenheit (-20 degrees Celsius), snowfall becomes unlikely in most places."

The temperature must be below freezing for ice crystals to attach to each other and drift down to earth. But when the temperatures are extremely, insanely low, the ice crystals do not hook up. There can be precipitation under extremely cold conditions, but it isn't considered snow. The common name for the stuff falling from the sky on a brutally cold day is ice needles. It happens pretty often in the Arctic, where such precipitation is called an ice fog.

TORNADOES CANNOT CROSS A RIVER

How True Is It?
That's some twister-ed logic.

Awesome, erratic, and very, very dangerous, tornadoes have fascinated people even before the legendary twister struck Kansas in *The Wizard of Oz*. And as tends to be the case with such a powerful force of nature, a lot of mythology has grown up around tornadoes.

According to the *Glossary of Meteorology*, a tornado is "a violently rotating column of air ... often (but not always) visible as a funnel cloud" that has contact with both the ground and the clouds.

Local legends claim that certain places are safe because tornadoes peter out in a canyon, or cannot climb a hill or mountain, or cannot cross a river. According to Roger Edwards of the U.S. Storm Prediction Center, all these assertions are just plain wrong. At Salt Lake City, Utah, on August 11, 1999, a tornado went down one side of canyon and up another without losing its destructive power. In 1989 a tornado thundered up the Grand Teton Mountains, leaving a swath of destruction 60 miles long. Without a moment's hesitation, tornadoes have blown across the Mississippi and the Ohio Rivers. In fact, the deadliest tornado ever to strike the United States, the notorious Tri-State Tornado of March 18, 1925, roared across the Mississippi River from Missouri to Illinois. Before it was over, the tornado had taken the lives of 695 people.

Another old wives' tale says that tornadoes do not strike cities. Tell that to the citizens of St. Louis, Missouri, Topeka,

Kansas, Lubbock, Texas, and Denver, Colorado, all of which have seen tornadoes come roaring through their city streets.

Finally, there is the modern myth that tornadoes are drawn to trailer parks. First of all, and most obviously, tornadoes do not have intelligence, or personality, or any other faculty that would enable them to choose where to strike. According to Hampton Sides, editor of *Outside* magazine's "The Wild File" column, the impression that tornadoes go after trailer parks is based on the tragically high death toll among trailer residents when their park is hit. Because trailers are not built on a foundation, they are more likely to be torn apart or thrown about by the force of a tornado. That explains why, in 1994, 40 percent of all Americans who died in a tornado lived in a trailer—this in spite of the fact that trailers account for only 6 percent of housing in the United States.

Section Four

Swimmers Should Wait an Hour After Eating Before Going into the Water, and Other Old Wives' Tales About Sports

SWIMMERS SHOULD WAIT AN HOUR AFTER EATING BEFORE GOING INTO THE WATER

How True Is It?
Feel free to eat heartily, then take a dip in the drink.

Of all the horror stories told to children to keep them in line, one of the most persistent is the notion that any kid who does not wait an hour after eating before going into the water will develop a severe stomach cramp and drown. In 1956, the Red Cross manual included several pages in its water-safety section on the hazards of eating-then-swimming. The spread included a staged photo of a terrified victim about to go under.

Now, it is true that in the United States drowning ranks as the highest cause of accidental death among infants and children. But these poor kids did not drown because they scorned the one hour wait and raced from the picnic table straight into the swimming pool. Nonetheless, this old wives' tale endures.

The precise date is fuzzy, but we do know it was sometime in the 1930s when mothers and grandmothers first adopted the formula of Lunch + Swimming = Death as an article of faith. However, it is interesting to learn that back in 1956—the same year the alarmist edition of the Red Cross manual came out—B.W. Gabrielsen, the swimming coach at the University of Georgia, published the book *Facts on Drowning Accidents*. In it Coach Gabrielsen showed that jumping into the water after a meal led to fewer than 1 percent of all deaths by drowning, basically a statistical anomaly. In 1961 an exercise physiologist named Arthur Steinhaus concurred, publishing an article in the *Journal of*

Health, Physical Education, and Recreation in which he dismissed any link between eating lunch and then going swimming.

The digestion process breaks down food and liquid into small molecules of nutrients that can be absorbed by the cells and blood to nourish the body and provide energy. Swimming does not inhibit this natural process.

Even anecdotal evidence is against the old wives' tale. The website WrongDiagnosis.com, founded and maintained by patients, lists 63 causes for stomach cramps—from bowel obstruction to premenstrual discomfort to food poisoning. But swimming less than an hour after chowing down did not make the cut.

GOLF COURSES HAVE 18 HOLES BECAUSE A FIFTH OF SCOTCH WHISKEY CONTAINS 18 SHOTS

How True Is It?
Totally off the fairway.

Everybody knows that the Scots love golf, and the Scots love Scotch. Isn't it natural, then, that when designing the world's first golf course they would have based the number of holes on the number of shots contained in a standard-size bottle of Scotch whiskey?

The short answer is, "No." Think about it: who could possibly walk across the fairway, let alone hit a little white ball, with 18 shots of straight whiskey in his system? But logical explanations aside, there is also an historical one.

Although there has been a form of golf around at least since the days of the Romans, the number of holes on early golf courses differed vastly, even in Scotland. Scotland's Leith Links, for example, had only five holes, while the Montrose Links had 25.

Golfers have been playing at the internationally famous St. Andrews course—a narrow strip of land along the seashore—since the 15th century. The course originally had eleven holes that began virtually at the clubhouse door and stretched to the end of the property. You played the eleven holes out, then turned around and played the same holes back to the clubhouse. That made for a 22-hole game at St. Andrews.

Then, in 1764, the "Captain and Gentlemen Golfers," as the members of the St. Andrews club called themselves, decided that their first four holes were too short. They ordered them consolidated into just two holes, which transformed St. Andrews into an 18-hole golf game.

Standardization came slowly to golf. By 1882 two of the most prestigious golf clubs in the world—Prestwick and Muirfields—had 18-hole courses, which went a long way to making 18 holes the norm. Then, in 1897, The Royal and Ancient Golf Club of St Andrews was given authority to set the rules for golf. If ever there was an opportunity to make 18 holes official, this was it. Still, St. Andrews held back. It was not until 1950 that it was set down in the *Rules of Golf* that 18 holes was designated as a "stipulated round."

SPOUSAL ABUSE REACHES EPIDEMIC PROPORTIONS ON SUPER BOWL SUNDAY

How True Is It?
Not at all, thank goodness.

For once we can pinpoint exactly when a bit of folklore appeared: January 1993. The source was a media advocacy group, Fairness & Accuracy in Reporting (FAIR), that wanted to spotlight the problem of domestic violence against women by running a commercial during the Super Bowl. To convince NBC to give the commercial air-time, FAIR distributed a press release which stated that Super Bowl Sunday was "one of the worst days of the year for violence against women in the home." FAIR suggested that whether their team won or lost, the men watching the Super Bowl were so jacked up by the game that they had to find some way to release all their testosterone. The method many of these sports fans chose, according to FAIR, was beating their wives or girlfriends. To back up this claim, FAIR distributed another press release that said "women's shelters report a 40 percent increase in calls for help during Super Bowl Sunday."

That statistic—a 40 percent increase in domestic violence in a single day—attracted a lot of media attention. A couple of days before the Super Bowl representatives from several women's advocacy groups, along with representatives from FAIR, held a press conference in Pasadena, California, where the game was about to be played. Standing before the banks of microphones, Sheila Kuehl of the California Women's Law Center said that researchers at Old Dominion University in Virginia had found that after Washington Redskins' games, police reports and hospital admissions both showed a significant increase in reports of attacks on women.

Many news outlets accepted these figures at face value, running stories about "The Abuse Bowl." But *Washington Post* reporter Ken Ringle started investigating the claims. Domestic violence experts he spoke to said they had never seen a link between the Super Bowl and wife-beating. Ringle spoke with staff members at several women's shelters, none of whom said they saw a sudden surge on Super Bowl Sunday. Ringle even called Janet Katz, one of the authors of the Old Dominion study. Katz said that she had found that emergency room admissions of women who had been shot, stabbed, or otherwise injured on the days when the Redskins played was slightly higher than normal. But Katz insisted her study did not claim a 40 percent increase of violence against women.

So what does the Old Dominion study actually say? Over a two-year period hospital emergency rooms in northern Virginia saw 680 women who had been assaulted—that's less than one a day. What comes next sounds weird, but remember, we're dealing with statistics: on a normal day a Northern Virginia hospital emergency room expected to see 0.58 women who had been victims of violence; on a day when the Redskins played, they actually saw 0.80 battered women. That figures out to a 40 percent increase. Cecil Adams of *The Chicago Reader*, dug a little deeper and found that the "40 percent increase" translated into six cases of domestic violence in Northern Virginia—which is distressing, but not a sign of an emerging national crisis.

MAGNETS HEAL SPORTS INJURIES FASTER THAN CONVENTIONAL MEDICINE

How True Is It?
You're not really gonna fall for this, are you?

Periodically over the last 500 years someone has come along to tout the "miraculous" healing properties of the humble magnet. The first was the 16th-century alchemist/physician Paracelsus, who saw how a magnet could draw to itself metal objects that were some distance away and concluded—wrongly—that anything that powerful must have powerful healing properties, too.

One hundred years later an English charlatan, Dr. Robert Fludd, claimed that he could cure any ailment with his magnets, provided the patient remained in the "boreal position"—with his head pointing north and his feet pointing south—while the magnets worked their magic.

The most famous proponent of magnetism was Franz Mesmer (whose name gave us the word "mesmerize"). He came from Vienna to Paris in 1778, where he "healed" people by having them sit around a vat of what he described as "magnetized water" while holding iron rods in their hands. King Louis XVI asked Antoine Lavoissier, the founder of modern chemistry, and Benjamin Franklin, who was in Paris at the time as the ambassador for the American colonies, to look into Mesmer's methods. They found that the only power Mesmer and his magnets exerted was the power of suggestion.

In the late 1990s magnets became fashionable again, this time among professional athletes and weekend warriors. Miami

Dolphins quarterback Dan Marino reportedly used magnets to speed up the healing process when he broke an ankle, and Yankee center fielder Bernie Williams used them for an injured hamstring, while pro golfer Bob Murphy admitted to having magnets strapped all over his body as an antidote to growing old.

In a "Health Report" segment broadcast on ABC World News Tonight on August 11, 1997, telejournalist Juju Chang reported that healing magnets had become a multimillion-dollar business, and that sets of healing magnets were being sold at $89 a pop. The news report featured a series of therapeutic magnet experts who explained the power of magnetism. One claimed that magnetism can alter human tissue. Another said that "every human cell has a positive and a negative side to it." A third claimed that magnets draw more blood to an injured area, and that magnets can do this because blood contains iron.

In *Voodoo Science: The Road from Foolishness to Fraud*, physicist Robert L. Park tackled all of these claims regarding the health benefits of magnets. First, it is a biological impossibility for magnets to alter tissue. Second, human cells do not have positive and negative sides. Third, magnets do not draw blood to an afflicted area of the body, and you can make a test of this assertion at home. Apply a heating pad to any part of your body. Soon that area becomes flushed, or red, because the blood is being drawn to the overheated area to cool it down. Now strap a magnet to some part of your body. Nothing happens. No flushing. No redness. Why? Because the iron in blood molecules are in a chemical state, they aren't microscopic splinters of metal floating around in your blood stream that can be drawn by a magnet.

Finally, Park performed a simple test with these therapeutic magnets to see how strong they were. He found that the magnets in a therapeutic magnet kit he purchased could hold nine sheets of ordinary paper to the side of his steel file cabinet. When Park added a tenth sheet, however, the magnet's force couldn't penetrate the paper and everything fell to the floor.

Ten sheets of paper is just one millimeter thick. Even if magnets worked, they would barely penetrate the skin, which ranges in thickness from .05 millimeter on the eyelid to 4 millimeters on the soles of the feet. So it is impossible that the "force" of the magnets could reach down into torn muscle or broken bones.

IT'S BAD LUCK TO CHANGE A BOAT'S NAME

How True Is It?
It doesn't hold water.

No less an authority than Robert Louis Stevenson defended the practice of never changing a boat's name. In his 1881 novel *Treasure Island*, he tells of a seaman who tempted fate by changing the names of his ships and ended up "hanged like a dog."

According to the old folklore, changing a boat's name is like changing a person's name—it's bad form, plain and simple. Furthermore, just as a child receives its name at baptism, the ship receives its name in a christening ceremony. The way the old seadogs see it, to dispense with one name and adopt another is to tempt Providence.

In our own day, less orthodox types also warn against changing a boat's name. Numerologists, for example, claim that each letter of a name possesses a numerical equivalent with a unique corresponding energy. These various energies endow the boat with a kind of mystical or guardian force. To cancel the original name and take up a new one would scramble the boat's energy and could cause no end of trouble to the boat and its owner.

Boating writer John Vigor has come up with a Boat Denaming Ceremony in which the boat owner invokes the permission of Neptune, god of the sea, and Aeolus, god of the winds, before renaming the boat. The bottle of champagne smashed or sprayed against the boat when it receives its new name is offered as a libation to the seafarer's gods.

That said, the author of an article on the protocol for renaming a boat admits that a boating friend of his owned 24 yachts and renamed each one. Sounds risky, yet the yachtsman was never beset by pirates, nor shipwrecked, nor attacked by a vengeful white whale.

THE TYPE OF BASEBALL BAT A PLAYER SWINGS CAN MAKE OR BREAK HIS CAREER

How True Is It?
It's all in the eye of the bat holder.

American baseball players are a superstitious lot—arguably the most superstitious of all professional athletes. And they take their bats very seriously.

Some professional ball players will tell you always to spit in your hand before picking up your bat. To take your bat to bed with you. To talk nicely to your bat. And for heaven's sake, never loan your own bat to another teammate.

The quest for a winning baseball bat—like the Excalibur-esque "Wonder Boy" that appears in Bernard Malamud's novel, *The Natural*—is eternal in baseball. And if a winning bat is baseball's Holy Grail, then Louisville, Kentucky (home of the famous "Louisville Slugger"), is Jerusalem.

Every year Ted Williams of the Boston Red Sox made the trek to Louisville to search through the wood piles of the Hillerich and Bradsby Company. Williams, with a lifetime average of .344, insisted that his bats had to be made of wood with the narrowest grain. Al Simmons, famous for his unusual batting stance (he pointed his left foot way out toward left field) also traveled to Louisville, but he wanted a bat made from a piece of wood with the widest possible grain. He has a .334 lifetime average.

Eddie Collins (a Chicago White Sox infielder who came through the 1919 "Black Sox" scandal unscathed) went to Louisville to have bats made of half white wood and half red wood. After 25 seasons of swinging with bicolored bats, Collins retired with a lifetime batting average of .333.

So, what is it that makes a run-of-the-mill slugger a candidate for the Hall of Fame? Is it the spit? The grain? The color? The sweet-talking to the bat? Sports psychologist Richard Lustberg says, "Athletes... want to believe that their particular routine is enhancing their performance. In reality, it's probably just practice and confidence that's making them perform better."

Section Five

You Can Tell the Length of a Man's Penis by Checking Out His Shoe Size, and Other Old Wives' Tales of the Ways of Love

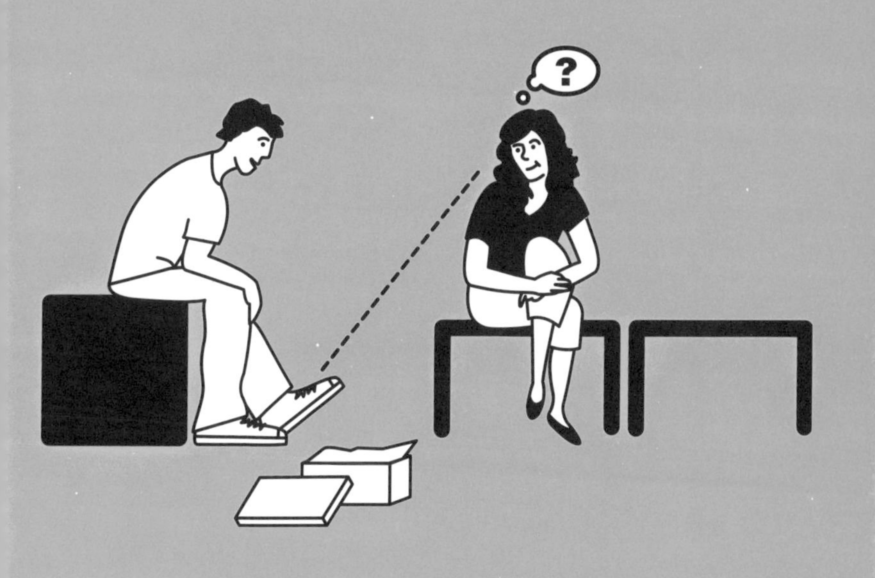

YOU CAN TELL THE LENGTH OF A MAN'S PENIS BY CHECKING OUT HIS SHOE SIZE

How True Is It?
You know what they say: big shoes ... big feet.

In ancient times, when everyone wore clothes in public and Speedos had not yet been invented, women wondered if there was some way to predict the size of a potential partner's package without actually having the guy undress. The old wives of the day insisted that there was a direct correlation between a man's shoe size and the length of his manhood.

This particular old wives' tale is especially popular with guys walking around in size 13 shoes. But is there any scientific data to back it up? It stands to reason, right? If a guy is big, everything on him will be big.

Researchers at University College London and urologists at London's St. Mary's Hospital, took it upon themselves to settle the shoe-size-indicates-penis-size question once and for all.

Eager to advance the frontiers of medical science, 104 volunteers, ranging in age from adolescent boys to elderly men, submitted their feet and their johnsons to the merciless precision of modern measurement devices. To ensure that there would be no discrepancies, each volunteer was examined concurrently by two urologists. The urologists measured each penis when flaccid and again when gently stretched. Length was recorded to the nearest 0.5 centimeter. The urologists also noted the subject's age and, of course, his shoe size.

After an exhaustive analysis of their data, the researchers published their findings in the *British Journal of Urology*

International. The authors of the British study concluded, "The ability to predict the size of a man's penis by observing his shoe size is a common misconception; the present study shows that there is no scientific support for the relationship."

Naturally, the results didn't please everyone, including the urologists involved in the study, one of whom was quoted by the Reuters health news service as complaining, "There must be some part of the body that is predictive of penile length."

OPPOSITES ATTRACT

How True Is It?
The opposite is true.

Two people of wildly different backgrounds and interests meet and are smitten. Confronted with the depth and the intensity of their love, all conventional obstacles melt away. This is the basic plot of Lord knows how many myths, folk tales, romance novels, and Hollywood movies. The supposed truism that opposites attract is so ingrained in our society that people who are brave enough to deride it out loud and in public are written off as cranks and cynics.

As is often the case, the cranks and the cynics got it right. For love—and even just for a roll in the hay—like seeks out like. Take a look at the data collected by the 1994 *Sex in America Survey*.

Let's start with race. Although today interracial couples find greater acceptance in American society than in years past, 94 percent of sexually active unmarried white men pair up with white women. In terms of other racial groups, 2.1 percent of white men have a Hispanic partner, 1.9 percent have an Asian partner, while only 0.6 percent have an African-American partner.

As for sexually active unmarried white women, 89.5 percent have a white partner, 6.4 percent have an African-American partner, 1.6 percent have a Hispanic partner, and only 0.7 percent have an Asian partner.

You can find the same pattern among African-Americans: 82 percent of black men choose a black woman as their partner, 7.6 percent have a white partner, and 4.6 percent have a Hispanic partner.

Among sexually active unmarried black women, an incredible 97 percent choose black men, while only 1 percent have a white partner and 1 percent an Asian partner.

But race is not the only factor. The pattern holds true in other areas, too. For example, both men and women tend to have sex with partners who have their same level of education. Seventy-eight percent of men who never graduated high school only hooked up with women whose formal education stopped at high school.

Men who graduated from college also tended to look for love among other college graduates. Eight percent wandered farther afield by dating a woman with a graduate degree, but only 2 percent went to bed with a woman who had not finished high school. The rest enjoyed meetings of the mind.

Women were just as predictable: 81 percent of women who had no high school diploma paired up with men whose academic careers ended at high school. Seventy-one percent of women who had graduate degrees limited their field to men who had at least a bachelor's degree. None of the women with advanced degrees in the *Sex in America* sample slept with a man who had not finished high school.

Even religious affiliation mattered. Contrary to what the 1960s sitcom, "Bridget Loves Bernie," told us, nice Catholic girls are not likely to marry nice Jewish boys. Even for premarital sex, 68 percent of Catholic men hook up with Catholic women. On the other side of the coin, the number is almost identical: 67 percent of Catholic women choose Catholic men.

Among Protestant men, 61 percent pair up with Protestant women, and 72 percent of Protestant women look for love among Protestant men.

The results of study not only overturn centuries of romantic hogwash, it also pretty much blows out of the water the cherished

American notion that in our personal lives we are not confined to the old ghettoes of race and class, religion and education. When we go hunting for a partner, our overwhelming tendency is to look for someone who reminds us a lot of ourselves.

COLD HANDS, WARM HEART

How True Is It?
It's the truth, hands-down.

Folklore assures us that women with cold hands have very warm hearts. Though there haven't been any studies showing a correlation between body temperature and a predisposition toward kindness, the literal interpretation of the assertion has been investigated. And according to the latest scientific evidence, the old wives got it right.

At the University of Utah Dr. Joseph Lyon and his team of graduate students recruited 219 individuals—141 women and 78 men—ranging in age from infants to seniors in their eighties, for this unusual experiment.

The research began as a hunch. Lyon was working at an urgent-care facility when he thought he felt a pattern in patient skin temperature: women felt cooler to the touch than men. As an early test of his intuition, Lyon measured a nurse's skin temperature and then measured his own. The nurse's temperature came in at 75 degrees Fahrenheit (23.87 Celsius); Lyon's registered 95 degrees Fahrenheit (34.97 Celsius).

Soon Lyon and his graduate students were collecting volunteers and taking readings of the temperature of the fingernails of their subjects' left and right middle fingers. To record their measurements the research team used ultrasensitive infrared tympanic thermometers. The results found that on average a woman's hands are 2.8 degrees Fahrenheit (1.55 Celsius) cooler than a man's hands. But, short of surgery, how do you measure the warmth of a human heart?

That's when the muse visited Lyon and his students for the second time: they realized that they could establish the core body temperature of every volunteer by measuring both eardrums. The result: on average the women's hearts tested at 97.8 degrees Fahrenheit (36.52 Celsius) while the hearts of men averaged a cooler 97.4 degrees Fahrenheit (36.3 Celsius).

At first glance the whole project sounds like a lark, but Dr. Lyon believes that the cold hands, warm heart experiment could lead to useful medical information. He and his team are planning to study whether people with cold hands have more trouble with arthritis and cardiovascular disease.

EATING POWDERED RHINOCEROS HORN IMPROVES A MAN'S VIRILITY

How True Is It?
That's not what people mean when they say, "horny."

When Westerners are in the market for an aphrodisiac, they head for the oyster bar. In Asia, however, the two top aphrodisiacs are tiger penis and rhinoceros horn. Both are the subjects of wishful thinking. True, a tiger is a powerful animal, but his strength is not concentrated in his penis. And a rhino's horn may resemble a huge phallus, but all it is really is a dense compound of hair and keratin, the stuff that makes fingernails.

Recently scientists in Malaysia have been studying a less exotic aphrodisiac—a plant known as tongkat ali (or *eurycoma longifolia Jack*, to use its scientific name). The tongkat ali plant grows wild in Southeast Asia, with the highest concentrations in Indonesia. And, unlike the tiger's penis or the rhino's horn, there is evidence to suggest that tongkat ali really does rev up a man's libido and improve his sexual prowess.

To test the plant's effects, Dr. Ismail Tambi of the Human Reproduction Specialist Centre at Malaysia's National Population and Family Development Board, assembled 30 healthy men between the ages of 31 and 52. Each man took two capsules of tongkat ali every day for three weeks. At the end of the study, the men reported that the tongkat ali had a marked influence on their sexual performance: they experienced erections that were stronger and lasted longer. But Dr. Tambi did not rely solely on this anecdotal evidence. He had measured the

The United States Food and Drug Administration Weighs in on Aphrodisiacs

For at least 5,000 years humans have put their faith in the effectiveness of everything from anchovies and licorice to ginseng and yohimbine to improve their love life. Do any of these foods and herbs deserve their reputation?

According to the FDA, the answer is yes and no. Oysters, for example, have a reputation in the West as a love aid. It's said that to maintain his credentials as 18th-century Europe's greatest lover, Casanova slurped down 50 oysters a day. It's true that oysters are rich in zinc, and that more zinc in the diet can improve one's sex drive, so maybe Casanova was on to something.

Then there is the bark of Africa's yohimbine tree, which has been the aphrodisiac of choice for centuries in Africa and West India, where they say it activates the nerve centers that induce an erection. The FDA has tested the effects of yohimbine on laboratory animals and pronounced the results "encouraging." But the researchers also warn that these early results do not mean that yohimbine really does everything its advocates claim.

The word ginseng means "man root," and the plant does look like a figure of a man. In China, Tibet, Korea, Southeast Asia, and India ginseng is used not only as a sexual stimulant, but also a rejuvenation tonic. So far, however, no study has concluded that ginseng really does improve one's sex life.

If the data doesn't back up these magic potions, why have people put their faith in them for so many centuries? John Renner, founder of the Consumer Health Information Research Institute, believes the effectiveness of aphrodisiacs is all in our heads. "The mind is the most potent aphrodisiac there is," he said. "It's very difficult to evaluate something someone is taking because if you tell them it's an aphrodisiac, the hope of a certain response might actually lead to an additional sexual reaction."

level of testosterone in his subjects at the outset of the experiment. Now he measured the men's testosterone level again and found that after taking tongkat ali for three weeks, their testosterone levels had doubled.

Of course, testosterone is almost as desirable in the gym as it is in the bedroom. Testosterone reduces body fat, increases muscle strength, and builds muscle mass. But it seemed like too much to ask that tongkat ali could double as an aphrodisiac and as a fat-burning, muscle-building elixir.

In 2003 researchers at the Department of Exercise Physiology Sports Centre at Malaysia's University of Malaya brought in fourteen healthy men to follow a rigorous workout program over a five-week period. Seven of the men received the tongkat ali extract (100 mg per day), while the other seven received a placebo.

The British Journal of Sports Medicine reported the results of the study. There were insignificant changes in terms of body fat, increased muscle strength, and increased muscle mass among the seven men who received the placebo. For the seven men who received the tongkat ali extract, however, the results were incredible. In just five weeks their body fat went down almost a full percentage point, their muscle strength increased by 6.78 percent, and their muscle mass increased by 5 percent. As if that weren't enough, the average size of their biceps grew 1.8 centimeters, or almost a full inch.

No wonder tongkat ali extract has become such a hot topic of discussion in gyms and health clubs.

AFTER SEX, IF A MAN WASHES HIS PENIS WITH ALOE VERA, HE WON'T CONTRACT SEXUALLY TRANSMITTED DISEASES

How True Is It?
Your health teacher was right: the only safe sex is no sex.

Aloe vera is an effective medicine for burns, insect bites, and skin rashes such as poison ivy. The ancient Egyptians were using the balm from this spiky plant for all of these ailments 4500 years ago.

But as good as aloe vera is, it has its limits. Contrary to a myth current on the Caribbean island of Tobago, a man can not protect himself against sexually transmitted diseases by washing his penis with aloe vera after he has had sex. Nonetheless, in the 1990s a Baltimore businessman conned approximately 3,700 people into buying an aloe vera magic potion that he said would cure herpes, cancer, and even AIDS. The product, called T-Up, was a mixture of aloe vera and cesium chloride, a compound that can set off an irregular heartbeat in animals. Needless to say, the United States Food and Drug Administration never approved T-Up as either a cancer or an AIDS treatment. Yet between April 1997 and October 1998, the company raked in $2.3 million from ailing, desperate people who fell for the pitch that T-Up was a miracle drug.

The claims of alternative medicine have rarely been hashed out in an American courtroom, but Maryland's State Attorney General J. Joseph Curran Jr., and its state consumer protection chief, William Leibovici, agreed that T-Up, Inc. was not marketing some harmless herbal elixir, but was engaged in fraud.

This consumer protection case went to trial in the U.S. District Court in Baltimore in April 2000. While the trial was in progress, the Consumer Protection Division levied a $3.7 million fine against the company that sold T-Up and ordered the company to reimburse the patients or their families. The trial ended in September 2001 when T- UP's president, Allen J. Hoffman, pleaded guilty to two counts of distributing his aloe vera potion with intent to defraud the public.

MEN THINK ABOUT SEX EVERY FIFTEEN SECONDS

How True Is It?
How could anyone get anything done if this were true?

Everybody knows that men are obsessed with sex. Common knowledge assures us that men have a randy thought every fifteen seconds. There's another version that says men are actually in a naughty state of mind every seven seconds. The number may differ, but the basic assertion is that men are essentially wanton beasts. And if the old wives are right about this, you can't help but wonder how much more men like Julius Caesar, Michelangelo, Thomas Edison, and Albert Einstein could have accomplished if their concentration hadn't been interrupted every few seconds by an impure thought.

Naturally, it is difficult to pin down exactly how often the average guy thinks about sex. Perhaps it is best, then, to turn to a source that is generally regarded as definitive on the subject of human sexuality, *Sexual Behavior in the Human Male*, better known as the Kinsey Report.

According to the FAQ section of the Kinsey Institute Web site, when men were asked, "How often do you think about sex?" 54 percent answered that they think about sex every day or several times a day; 43 percent said they think about sex a few times per month or a few times per week; and 4 percent replied that thoughts of sex cross their minds less than once a month. Compared to the seven-second or even the fifteen-second rule, these results are disappointing.

But what about women? Assuming the ladies were being honest and not merely modest, only 19 percent admitted to thinking about sex every day or several times a day; a whopping 67 percent said they thought about sex only a few times per month or a few times per week; and 17 percent said they had a sexual thought less than once a month.

Interestingly, the 1994 *Sex in America Survey* found that, contrary to conventional wisdom, the men and women who thought about sex most often were not sad sacks who couldn't get a date. The ones with the most active fantasy lives also had the most active sex lives.

DOG MEAT BOOSTS A MAN'S VIRILITY

How True Is It?
Leave poor Fido alone.

Strange items appear on just about every nation's menu. The French eat snails in garlic butter. The Italians make black pasta from squid ink. And the Koreans eat dogs.

In the West, where dogs are regarded almost universally as beloved pets, the notion of serving a pooch as an entree is horrific. But not so everywhere. A 2002 report estimates that about 3 million of South Korea's 47 million people eat dog meat regularly. Furthermore, Korea has about 6,000 restaurants nationwide that specialize in serving dog.

In Korea dog meat is regarded as a health-giving delicacy. A favorite preparation is *poshintang*, which means "body preservation stew." According to Korean folklore, the hot, humid days of summer sap the body of its strength and vitality. Dog meat is said to restore your natural vigor. Traditional Chinese medicine—which is widely practiced in Korea—backs up this belief, insisting that dog meat is not only ideal on a sweltering day, it is also an excellent restorative for the sick.

And dog meat is said to have an extra benefit: the hormones found in dog meat increase a man's virility. There is no scientific data to support such a claim. In fact, there is no scientific data to support any of the supposed benefits of dining on dog meat.

During the 1988 Summer Olympics at Seoul, the Korean government, worried about its image in front of a global audience, shut down the country's dog restaurants—a move that many Koreans viewed as a shameless attempt to pander to visitors who were likely to regard this aspect of traditional Korean culture as unsavory. For the month-long 2002 World Cup soccer finals, however, the Korean government showed itself to be less squeamish. The dog restaurants stayed open.

YOU CAN'T GET PREGNANT IN A HOT TUB

How True Is It?
Oh yes you can.

A new crop of old wives—most of them students on college campuses across the United States—believe that it isn't necessary to use a contraceptive when having sex in a hot tub because the heat of the water will kill the guy's sperm. A variant on this old wives' tale says that you can't catch any sexually transmitted disease in a hot tub.

It makes you wonder, how did these people get into college?

So let's tackle right away the essential issue in this old wives' tale. Most hot tubs are set at a temperature of 104 degrees Fahrenheit. In order to act as a spermaticide or an antibiotic the water in a hot tub would have to be at an absolutely scalding temperature (at least 120 degrees Fahrenheit)—much too hot for anyone to soak in, let alone fool around. So yes, you can get pregnant in a hot tub, and you can catch an STD in a hot tub.

Still, there is a link between hot tubs and sperm production. Testicles are sensitive to heat. And if a guy spends a lot of time sitting in a hot tub this exposure to high temperatures will lower his sperm production. Please note: the hot tub is not killing off the sperm, nor is it making the man sterile; it is just lowering sperm production. And after soaking in hot tubs on a regular basis, it takes a while for the sperm factory to return to producing at its normal capacity again—a minimum of three months, according to malereproduction.com.

But men aren't the only ones who should think twice before climbing into a hot tub. Bacteria and even the cleaning solutions used in communal hot tubs such as the kind we find at health clubs or spas can cause health problems. The elderly and anyone with a low immune system runs the risk of picking up a skin rash, an ear infection, even pneumonia or Legionnaire's disease in a public hot tub. Newly pregnant women should steer clear of hot tubs, too. Raising a pregnant woman's core body temperature during the first 28 days of pregnancy can put the unborn child at risk of poor spinal development.

Section Six

Walking Under a Ladder Is Bad Luck, and Other Old Wives' Tales to Keep You Safe

Warning

Falling objects

WALKING UNDER A LADDER IS BAD LUCK

How True Is It?
True enough that you should take those extra steps and walk around.

The old wives' tale that it is bad luck to walk under a ladder is one of those stories that brings together superstition and common sense. The oldest roots of the superstition may go back to the early centuries of Christianity. A ladder leaning against a wall makes a triangle, and a triangle is a symbol of the Holy Trinity. To walk under a ladder, then, is to desecrate the symbol that represents the Father, the Son, and the Holy Spirit, and to align yourself with the devil.

But there is a problem with the logic of this superstition. The symbol of the Holy Trinity is an equilateral triangle in which all three sides are of equal length because all three Persons of the Trinity are equal. But a ladder leaning against a wall creates a right-angled triangle in which the three sides are of unequal length. In terms of the theology of the Trinity, this type of triangle is flagrantly heretical. So, one could interpret walking under a ladder as a symbolic poke in the eye to heresy.

Theological hair-splitting aside, the ladder superstition lives on. A 2003 study conducted in the United Kingdom found that refusal to walk under a ladder is the third most commonly held superstition, right behind knocking on wood (first place) and crossing one's fingers (second place).

Now, while it is true that a stroll under a ladder will not endanger your soul, the potential dangers to your body are alarming. The American Academy of Orthopedic Surgeons has found that 500,000 people in the United States are treated for ladder-related injuries every year. Furthermore, approximately 300 of these injuries prove to be fatal. The United Kingdom sees over 40,000 ladder accidents annually, and about 50 ladder-related deaths.

Accidents range from those caused by ladders that have been placed on an unstable surface to ladders set against a wall at an unsafe angle; from climbers who are up too high and lose their balance or fall because their shoes are slick with grease or mud, to dropped buckets and tools that strike unwary passersby.

The Bureau of Labor Statistics in Sweden found that 80% of all ladder accidents involved a fall; 73% involved do-it-yourselfers who did not know how to use a ladder safely; 57% involved individuals who had been trying to climb the ladder while holding a tool or some other object in one or both hands; and 30% involved climbers who simply slipped and fell.

Clearly, the old wives were right: with all those ladders collapsing, climbers falling, and tools, buckets, and all manner of paraphernalia dropping to the ground, only a fool would walk under a ladder.

IF YOU STICK YOUR TONGUE OUT, YOU WILL ABSORB MILLIONS OF GERMS AND BACTERIA

How True Is It?
True, but keeping it in your mouth isn't much better.

There is a kernel of truth to the old wives' tale that cautions us not to stick out our tongues lest millions of germs collect there. The tongue does attract bacteria, but not because you were so rude as to stick it out of your mouth.

The bacteria on your tongue are called anaerobic, which means that they live in a mostly oxygen-free environment, i.e., your mouth. Floating around in there are dead cells from the lining of your mouth as well as tiny food particles. The anaerobic bacteria break these things down from solids into gases that smell pretty bad. The formal name for these gases is "volatile sulphur compounds," or VSC. Stand in front of a mirror and open your mouth. See that white stuff at the back of your tongue? That is VSC. The gases often get caught amid the tiny lumps and minuscule crevices of your tongue's taste-buds, where they become concentrated, resulting in bad breath, or halitosis, to use the clinical term.

To get rid of the bad breath you have to get rid of the VSC. Simply brushing your teeth won't do it. Neither will swishing some over-the-counter mouthwash around the inside of your mouth. (By the way, did you know that the mouthwash industry rakes in $850 million in sales a year? That's a lot of money for a product that is essentially ineffective.)

According to Dr. Barry Cash, a dentist at the Fresh Breath

Center in Toronto, Canada, most patients will have to use a tongue scraper regularly to remove the foul-smelling debris that collects at the back of the tongue, and apply a prescription gel to the tongue at night. The gel prevents dry mouth during the night thereby keeping the tongue oxygenated and promoting the production of saliva.

So when it comes to germs and your tongue, it's not the stuff you might inhale that you should worry about: it's the bacteria that are already percolating at the back of your mouth that might make other people groan when you exhale.

IF YOU KILL A COBRA, ITS MATE WILL COME AFTER YOU

How True Is It?
Don't be hiss-terical.

In India the old wives say that if you kill a cobra, make sure you dispose of the body far from your home. Otherwise the mate will see your reflection locked in the dead cobra's eyes and come looking for you.

The idea that some animals have human intelligence and will come after us shows up in folklore across the world. It's even made its way in classic literature (Herman Melville's novel of a vengeful white whale, *Moby Dick*) and blockbuster movies (Steven Spielberg's film of a giant man-stalking shark, *Jaws*).

It is true that some wild animals are man-hunters: grizzly bears and tigers have been known to go after humans who invade their habitats. Cobras, however, do not hunt people. And that's just the first thing that's off-base about this particular old wives' tale.

Next there is the question of the picture in the dead cobra's eyes. Eyes are not cameras. They do not store images of what they've seen—not even the picture of the person who killed the eyes' owner. Besides, a cobra does not use its eyes to hunt; the cobra uses its sense of smell which is concentrated not in the nostrils but in the cobra's long tongue. By flicking out its tongue, the cobra gets a sense of what is in the neighborhood.

Then there is the revenge question. If you did something to make a cobra feel endangered, it will retaliate by trying to bite you. But we're talking about a direct cause-and-effect situation. Let's say you take a swing at a cobra with a stick. You miss. It strikes out at you. It misses. You run back to the house; the cobra slinks off into the grass. Back in its lair the cobra is not nursing a grudge, waiting for the day when it can finally nail you and pump 350 milligrams of venom into your blood stream.

Finally, we come to the issue of the cobra's mating habits. Unlike beavers, cobras do not mate for life. During mating season male cobras compete for a female. Once a male and female have paired up, the female makes a nest in which she lays between 30 and 50 eggs. During the three months it takes for the eggs to hatch, the male stays close to the nest, ready to kill any predator that comes near. Once the cobra hatchlings emerge, the male cobra slithers away. Cobras possess no sense of family loyalty.

BABY SNAKES ARE MORE POISONOUS THAN ADULTS

How True Is It?
Don't be deceived by the small package—they pack a powerful punch.

Humans are hard-wired to be terrified of snakes. But could the idea that baby snakes pack a more poisonous punch than their Mommy or Daddy be just an extension of our fundamental reptile phobia?

Actually, no. The old wives have got the story right: baby snakes really are more deadly than adult snakes. When a newborn venomous snake slithers out of its egg, it is equipped with poison that is more potent than that of its parents.

Snake experts are not entirely certain why this should be the case. One theory holds that because the baby snakes haven't bitten anything yet their system has not had to regenerate more poison; thus, their venom is at full strength and much more dangerous. Another theory suggests that a high percentage of water is found in the venom of baby snakes which enables the poison to be absorbed more quickly into the victim's bloodstream.

On the bright side, a baby snake isn't as practiced as an adult at hurling itself at a victim—so it might miss you! And the baby snake's venom sac is smaller than a adult's, so the amount of venom injected into a victim is smaller. Nonetheless, as Hampton Sides, editor of *Outside* magazine's "The Wild File" column, has found, a bite from a tiny baby diamondback rattlesnake can dissolve your tissue and leave a nasty permanent scar. And a baby copperhead has enough venom to burn right through your tissue down to the bone.

If you are so unfortunate as to run across a nest of baby snakes, be afraid. And get out of there fast.

Section Seven

To Get the Marriage Off on the Right Foot, Carry the Bride Across the Threshold, and Other Old Wives' Tales of Marriage

TO GET THE MARRIAGE OFF ON THE RIGHT FOOT, CARRY THE BRIDE ACROSS THE THRESHOLD

How True Is It?
Only reassures the superstitious.

In parts of Mexico the threshold of the bride's parents' house is the scene of an unusual drama. On the day of the wedding the bride pretends that she's had a change of heart, that she's decided her groom is not worthy of her. So the groom goes to the bride's house, where she waits just inside the threshold with her mother, her sisters, and her other female relatives. Once the groom arrives all the women make him sing, dance, and perform tricks before they agree that he is worthy after all and the marriage can go forward.

The oldest version of the threshold superstition goes back to ancient Rome. Just as a Mexican bride feigns to have lost interest in her groom, a newlywed Roman bride would refuse to cross the threshold of her new home to show that she was a modest, well-brought-up young woman reluctant to give up her virginity. She would only surrender her scruples after the groom lifted her up and carried her into the house.

The most widely known version of the threshold superstition comes from Scotland, where carrying the bride across the threshold of her new home was an early form of marriage insurance. Witches were said to place curses on the newlyweds' threshold to trip the bride as she crossed and thus kick off a lifetime of bad luck and marital misery. But the malevolence of the witch could be frustrated if the groom gallantly lifted his new wife across the doorsill and set her down safely inside the house.

10 Most Common Wedding Insurance Claims

1. Damage to wedding attire.
2. Photographs damaged or ruined.
3. Cancellation due to illness or bereavement in immediate family.
4. Caterer fails to turn up at the reception.
5. Lost wedding rings.
6. Wedding transport is a no-show.
7. Cancellation due to venue being double booked.
8. Property damage.
9. Lost or stolen wedding presents.
10. Supplier goes out of business.

from E&L Insurance, United Kingdom

The custom survives today as a quaint wedding tradition, although these days the groom is more likely to carry his bride across the threshold of the hotel room where they will spend the night before setting off on their honeymoon. But whatever its origin or modern equivalent, the old wives were just plain wrong about the threshold thing. Curses do not work, and demons and witches do not lurk at the entrance to houses, or apartments, or hotel rooms.

There are, however, plenty of real problems that can afflict a bride. And the way to ward off these disasters is appropriately modern: wedding insurance. Specialized insurance companies in the United States, the United Kingdom, and Australia offer policies that will cover just about everything except the bride or groom changing her or his mind.

Policies cover damage to the wedding dress, loss of the wedding rings, injury to guests, damage to the church or reception hall, even coverage for such catastrophes as the caterer failing to arrive or a natural disaster that postpones the wedding.

ON FEBRUARY 29, A WOMAN CAN ASK A MAN TO MARRY HER

How True Is It?
Like leap year, it happens occasionally.

A common thread in folklore around the world asserts that taking decisive action on an extraordinary day can have positive consequences. Since February 29 comes around only once every four years, many societies believed that it was an auspicious day for conceiving or birthing babies, proposing marriage, or getting married.

In Europe, especially in the British Isles, February 29 is the day when women no longer have to wait for men to get up the nerve to propose marriage: the ladies can pop the question themselves—without the risk of appearing ill-bred, or desperate. There are even bogus credentials for this custom. It's said that in 1228 Queen Margaret of Scotland decreed that any man who turned a woman down on February 29 would be fined £1. Another tradition, also from Scotland, says the Scots Parliament passed a law that if a man wouldn't marry the bold lassie who proposed to him, he had to make amends by giving her a silk gown or £100. And a third tradition says the right of women to pop the question is enshrined in English common law.

They sound delightfully Old World, but don't be fooled: all of these laws are mythical. It's all very colorful, but it's also all nonsense.

There is a version of this myth in the United States called Sadie Hawkins Day. The holiday is named for a marriage-mad female from Al Capp's cartoon strip, "L'il Abner." On Sadie

Hawkins Day, a gal can ask a feller to marry her. In the U.S., however, unlike other parts of the world, there is no official Sadie Hawkins Day. It can fall on any day of the calendar year. This has led to a tradition in high schools, the Sadie Hawkins Dance, in which the girls ask the boys for a date.

These days, the old wives' tale has become cutesified. But in the ancient world, it was common for Celtic women to pop the question (and they did not wait until leap year). Today it is perfectly acceptable for a woman to ask her boyfriend to marry. There is even a website, www.ehow.com, that offers women tips on how to set the mood and choose the perfect setting so their prospective groom will feel at ease and be inclined to say, "Yes!"

TO SEE A MAGPIE MEANS YOU'RE ABOUT TO MARRY

How True Is It?
Don't book the caterer just yet.

There are natural and supernatural reasons why the magpie is regarded as a bird of marriage, happiness, and good luck in China. Magpies sing beautifully. Hearing a flock of them singing together is one of life's little pleasures. No wonder that in traditional Chinese culture, to hear a magpie sing is a sign that happiness is on its way.

The Manchu Chinese regard the magpie as a sacred bird. A legend tells how the goddess Fokulon once saw a beautiful magpie with a red fruit in its mouth flying high above her. As the bird floated overhead it dropped the fruit. Fokulon picked it up, ate it, and soon found she was pregnant. She gave birth to a boy whom she named Bukulirongshun: he became the ancestor of the Manchus.

Another legend says that Bukulirongshun's descendant, a boy named Fancha, was on the run from killers out to massacre all the Manchus. Just as his pursuers were about to catch him, a magpie lighted on the boy's head, transforming him into a tree. After the murderers had run right by him, the magpie turned Fancha back into a boy again, thus saving the Manchu people.

The Manchus' high regard for the magpie as their personal patron of good luck only increased in 1644 when a Manchu became Emperor of China, founding the Qing Dynasty that endured until 1911.

The magpie's connection with marriage comes from another Chinese legend. Many years ago the emperor's youngest daughter fell desperately in love with a cowherd. When the emperor learned of the affair, he exiled the lovers to opposite ends of the sky, and ordered a vast band of stars to keep the cowherd and the princess apart. But a flock of magpies took pity on the lovers and built an enchanted bridge so the couple could be together forever.

It's a lovely story, but when we look at how magpies actually behave in nature, they are not an especially good model for marriage. Unlike swans that mate for life, magpies are social birds, generally living in groups that range in number from 3 to 24. This group is not a happy, extended family. It is a harem. Only one of the birds in the group is male, and he mates with all the females.

MEN HAVE ONE LESS RIB THAN WOMEN

How True Is It?
This tale comes up short.

In the Book of Genesis we read that after God had made Adam from clay, he said, "It is not good for man to be alone; let us make him a help like unto himself." So God cast a deep sleep upon Adam, removed one of Adam's ribs, then filled up the empty space in the rib cage with flesh. From this rib he made Eve. Ever since, men have had one less rib than women.

Of course, the Bible does not say that, after Adam, all his male descendants would be a rib short, but that hasn't stopped the old wives. So in 2004, Dallas, Texas's premier rib joint, Tony Roma's restaurant, conducted a survey among the rib-savvy members of its Tony Roma's Loyalty Club to see how many people believe in the men-are-one-rib-short story. Out of 9,428 respondents—men and women—47 percent thought the story was true.

To settle the issue Tony Roma's got in touch with Dr. Stephen Sapp, professor and chairman of the Department of Religious Studies at the University of Miami. Dr. Sapp explained that the removal of a bone, miraculously or surgically, does not cause a change in a person's genetic makeup that he would pass along to his offspring. To clarify the point, he made a simple analogy: to believe that because Adam lost a rib all his male descendants are a rib short is like believing that if you have your appendix removed, your children and all your descendants will be born without an appendix.

In case you are wondering, the human body has 12 pairs of ribs. That's standard equipment for both men and women.

THROWING RICE AT THE BRIDE AND GROOM BRINGS THEM GOOD LUCK

How True Is It?
The only thing it brings them is grains of rice in uncomfortable places.

The custom of showering newlyweds with grain is ancient. More than 2,000 years ago the Romans tossed grains of wheat at the bride and groom, wheat being a symbol of fertility and prosperity. A Roman bride reinforced the custom by wearing a garland of wheat in her hair, and carrying a small sheaf of wheat as a bridal bouquet. The Romans regarded the grains of wheat that bounced off the bride as especially lucky: unmarried girls scrambled to collect these grains to ensure that they would be the next to marry.

Perhaps because of the influence of the Roman Empire, the tradition of throwing wheat at a wedding became widespread across ancient Europe and survived through the Middle Ages. In the 16th century, during the reign of Queen Elizabeth I, the custom experienced an odd metamorphosis. Instead of showering wheat on the happy couple, wedding guests tossed tiny cakes at them. No one knows why the tradition changed. But we can guess why the cake-tossing tradition didn't last long. It had to be a messy affair.

During the 17th century, in place of throwing little cakes, the wedding guests were invited to eat a share of one large cake. This was undeniably tidier. Yet the impulse to sling something at a bride and groom is deeply rooted in the human race. And so by the 18th century the old tradition was revived with rice—cheap, readily available, and already bridal white by nature.

If prostitution is the world's oldest profession, selling wedding paraphernalia is probably the second. Today wedding supply companies sell heart-shaped rice. It's real rice that has been reconstituted into tiny hearts. The bridal supply website, www.bridesvillage.com, sells the stuff for $16.25 a bag.

No doubt some of our readers are repulsed by the thought of tossing uncooked white rice outdoors. "What about the birds?" they wail. At least since the 1990s a new old wives' tale has attached itself to this venerable wedding custom. According to this latest myth, the stomachs of wild birds cannot digest raw white rice. The grains puff up in the bird's stomach until the tiny creature explodes.

Who would fall for such nonsense? Millions of people—especially after the advice columnist (and one of the most gullible people on the planet) Ann Landers urged her readers in 1996 to think about our feathered friends. "Please encourage the guests to throw rose petals instead of rice," she said. "Rice is not good for the birds."

How To Be a Good Wedding Guest

Not all cultures throw rice. If you've been invited to a wedding overseas, this list will help you show up at the ceremony ready to fling the right stuff.

Czech Republic: dried peas
France: wheat
Greece: candied almonds
India: puffed rice and flower petals
Italy: coins, candy, dried fruit
Korea: nuts and dates
Mexico: red beads
North Africa: figs and dates
Turkey: candy

"This silly myth pops up periodically, and it is absolutely unfounded," said Mary Jo Cheesman of the USA Rice Federation. Given Ms. Cheesman's association with the USA Rice Federation, she may not be an entirely unbiased source. Nonetheless, she has some good arguments. She points out that wild birds feed in rice fields all the time. If raw rice eaten off the stalk doesn't make them blow up, why would raw rice that they pick up off the church steps do so?

Ornithologists dismiss the myth, too. Biologist Ned Johnson who lectures at the University of California at Berkeley on the care and feeding of birds, says "There is no reason why birds, including small songbirds, can't eat rice."

So at the next wedding you attend, let the rice fly.

SLEEPING IN BLUE SHEETS MAKES THE BRIDEGROOM VIRILE

How True Is It?
True blue? Perhaps more than you might think.

In some parts of Mexico the old wives insist that on their wedding night the happy couple should bed down in a set of blue sheets. The color is said to make the groom virile.

Can something as apparently random as the color of bed linen actually influence a new husband's performance? Maybe.

Marketing research firms found that consumers make up their minds about a product or a setting in less than 90 seconds. According to these researchers, consumers base anywhere between 62 percent and 90 percent of their judgment on color.

For example, Pantone, the company that printers and designers rely upon for the widest array of ink colors, has known for decades that the most effective posters, flyers, advertisements, etc. are printed in black type on yellow background. Time and again tests have shown that this color combination gets the highest scores for legibility, attracting the eye, and even sticking in the memory.

Then there is this unexpected bit of medical research from Washington State University: patients have a higher tolerance for pain, and recover more quickly using less prescription medication, when they recuperate in a room painted green or in a room that contains lots of green accents such as plants.

Have you noticed how many fast-food restaurants are decorated in a color scheme of reds, yellows, and oranges? There is a reason for it: color research has shown that such "hot" colors somehow prompt people to eat more quickly. Restaurants decorated in blues and greens encourage more leisurely dining.

Many jails have holding cells painted a shade known as Baker-Miller Pink (popularly known as Drunk Tank Pink). It is a shade that comes close to the color of bubble gum. Why such a color in a jail, of all places? Dr. Alexander Schauss, director of the American Institute for Biosocial Research in Tacoma, Washington, discovered that this shade of pink has a positive effect on angry and violent prisoners. "It's a tranquilizing color," Dr. Schauss said.

So what about blue sheets? Color researchers have found that blue can decrease the heart rate and have a calming effect. And a bridegroom who is calm and confident rather than tense and over-eager is likely to perform better.

Section Eight

Water Goes Down the Drain in Different Directions Depending on Which Hemisphere You're in, and Other Old Wives' Tales About Running a Household

Ehrlichs Theory
N
W
E
S

WATER GOES DOWN THE DRAIN IN DIFFERENT DIRECTIONS DEPENDING ON WHICH HEMISPHERE YOU'RE IN

How True Is It?
This one's false the world over.

It's said that in the Northern Hemisphere, water goes down the drain in a counterclockwise direction. In the Southern Hemisphere water goes down the drain in a clockwise direction. The reason, according to the old wives, is that the earth's rotation affects the direction in which water drains depending on which side of the Equator you're on.

But it is simply not true. Fred W. Decker, professor emeritus of oceanic and atmospheric science at Oregon State University, says, "Really, I doubt that the direction of the draining water represents anything more than an accidental twist given by the starting flow."

Robert Ehrlich, a physicist at George Mason University, says that even if there is anecdotal evidence of bathtubs draining in different directions, it isn't the pull of the earth's rotation that is the cause. "In your tub," says Dr. Ehrlich, "such factors as any small asymmetry of the shape of the drain will determine in which direction the circulation occurs. Even in a tub having a perfectly symmetric drain, the circulation direction will be primarily influenced by any residual currents in the bathtub left over from the time when it was filled."

Some old wives may object, arguing that the direction water swirls down a drain is determined by the Coriolis effect. But they're indulging in pseudoscience. The Coriolis effect doesn't determine which way water rushes down a drain; the Coriolis effect relates to an apparent force that, due to the Earth's rotation, deflects moving objects—like air currents or projectiles—to the right in the Northern Hemisphere and to the left in the Southern Hemisphere. It doesn't say anything about liquids.

But the old wives don't give up so easily. They have pointed out that cyclones in the Northern Hemisphere swirl about in a counterclockwise direction, while cyclones in the Northern Hemisphere rotate in a clockwise direction. Once again we turn to Dr. Ehrlich for an answer. He says that the direction a cyclone takes is the result of "interactions between moving masses of air and air masses moving with the rotating earth." Remember that a cyclone is an immense storm system that covers a large piece of territory. It stands to reason that the effects, or the pull, of the earth's rotation will be "much more pronounced when the circulation covers a larger area than would occur inside your bathtub."

IT'S BAD LUCK TO KILL A LADYBUG

How True Is It?
That's no way to treat a lady(bug).

If you lived in Europe during the Middle Ages you'd have to have been a fool to kill a ladybug. According to the folklore of the time, the ladybug was a favorite, a kind of earthly pet of the Virgin Mary (who is also known as Our Lady). Through the ladybug Mary was said to shower all kinds of graces on good people: fine clothes, jewels, gold, and healthy babies. That last is why in some parts of Italy the ladybug was called *commaruccia*, which means "the little midwife." Consequently, anyone who killed a ladybug could expect be on the bad side of the Virgin Mary for nine days.

While a ladybug is not likely to bring you gold, jewels, or offspring, it is a very useful little creature nonetheless. Gardeners especially should be kind to ladybugs wherever they find them: in the garden, in the greenhouse, or even in the home. Ladybugs eat aphids, which damage roses, mites which destroy new buds on flowers, mealy bugs which thrive in greenhouses, and white flies which attack house plants such as fuchsia. In vegetable gardens the ladybug targets the tomato worm, the cabbage moth and the broccoli worm.

If you have insect trouble in your garden or greenhouse, you can buy packages of live ladybugs from gardening mail order companies. It's easy to release them in an enclosed space such as a greenhouse. Releasing a cloud of ladybugs out in the garden is another matter. To encourage them to remain in the neighborhood, try this little trick: spray the package of ladybugs with a solution of water and any sugary soft drink, then spread them around your garden. The sticky solution will prevent them from flying away for a couple days—long enough for the ladybugs to realize that there are plenty of aphids, or mites, or tomato worms to dine on right where they are.

CLUB SODA REMOVES RED WINE STAINS

How True Is It?
This remedy works sometimes—but eat, drink, and be careful.

It's an article of faith among housekeepers that if someone spills red wine on the carpet or the tablecloth, you should dowse the area with club soda and the stain will come right up. According to the club-soda-and-red-wine folklore, it's the carbonation, the bubbles, in the club soda that makes the stain float miraculously away.

Writing in *Scientific American* magazine, Pete Wishnok, a chemist at the Massachusetts Institute of Technology, said that there was really nothing in club soda that would cause it to act as a stain remover. It's just water, carbon dioxide, and some salt. "It is weakly acidic," Professor Wishnok says, "so it might decolorize stains."

Drawing upon his own experience, Professor Wishnok believes that the secret is not the club soda but the fabric upon which the red wine has been sloshed. Dozens of times he has removed red wine successfully from his carpet. "Our carpet is a synthetic that absorbs stains slowly," Professor Wishnok explained, "so—if you get there quickly with lots of paper towels—the club soda simply acts as a carrier to help blot everything up. Water would probably work as well, but club soda is more fun."

When red wine was spilled on his tablecloth, the club soda was much less effective. Professor Wishnok concludes the reason is the tablecloth was made of natural fibers and not as thick as a carpet, so it absorbed the wine quickly.

MISTLETOE IS AN ANTIDOTE TO POISON

How True Is It?
This one's patently mistle-leading.

More than 2000 years ago the Celts of France and the British Isles believed that mistletoe was one of the most potent plants in the forest. Distilled in a liquid, or eaten fresh off the vine, mistletoe was thought to cure illness, boost fertility, and was just what the doctor ordered if you happened to have eaten something poisonous.

Nothing could be farther from the truth. Every part of the mistletoe is toxic. Eat just a few berries and your stomach will rebel. Eat many mistletoe berries and you could be in serious trouble. Mistletoe berries contain toxic proteins known as lectins; the leaves contain toxic amines. Both are lethal.

Although the medicinal reputation of mistletoe is a washout, it is a fascinating plant in many other respects. Mistletoe is a parasitic plant, which means it does not sprout out of the ground on its own. Rather, its sticky seeds—either windborne, or delivered via bird droppings—adhere to tree branches. From these seeds tiny roots burrow through the bark of the host until the roots reach the xylem, the inner tissue of the limb that conveys moisture and nutrients through the tree. Just as the xylem feeds the tree, it nourishes the mistletoe, too. A single mistletoe plant clinging to a healthy tree won't do much damage, but a tree that becomes the host to several mistletoe plants will die.

Because the Druids considered the plant an emblem of peace, delicate negotiations between warring Celtic tribes were held beneath the mistletoe. According to the rules, everyone present at the peace conference had to lay down his arms and keep a truce for 24 hours. After the Celts were converted to Christianity, mistletoe survived as an emblem of friendship and goodwill.

The custom of kissing under the mistletoe developed from these earlier customs. Since mistletoe was associated with peace and goodwill, it seemed natural to bring it indoors at Christmas, the season of "peace on earth, goodwill to men." Usually the mistletoe was hung over the doorway, where guests were greeted with a friendly kiss. At some point during the 18th century in England, for reasons that are impossible to pin down, it became permissible for unmarried men to kiss any unmarried woman who happened to be standing under the mistletoe.

IT'S BAD LUCK TO KILL A BEE

How True Is It?
Unless it's stinging you, leave it be.

You won't be forever accursed with bad luck by the insect gods if you swat a bee, but considering all the benefits a bee provides, it really is wiser to leave the little creature alone.

First, bees produce honey. For centuries before mankind figured out how to process cane sugar, honey was the world's primary sweetener. Although the market for honey has shrunk, it is still delicious.

Then there is the purely practical consideration: without pollination the world would be a wasteland. And the most industrious of nature's pollinators is the bee. It moves pollen from one plant to another so flowers, vegetables, and fruit can grow and spread. Gardeners learned long ago that keeping a beehive or two in the backyard is a virtual guarantee of a bumper harvest of fruits, vegetables, and flowers.

At San Francisco University Dr. Keith Slessor, a chemist, and Dr. Mark Winston, an entomologist, developed a synthetic pheromone that mimics the substance secreted by a queen bee to attract worker bees. Once the workers are under the queen's spell, so to speak, they work harder to collect more pollen. Commercial fruit growers found that when they sprayed Drs. Slessor and Winston's synthetic bee pheromone on their trees and plants during the flowering season, they saw a net profit increase of $1,400 per hectare for pears, $1,270 for highbush blueberries, and up to $6,340 per hectare for cranberries.

If you aren't inclined to keep a beehive, nor in the market for a barrel of synthetic bee pheromone, you can still attract bees to your garden. Plant colorful flowers in large clusters, and sow sweet-smelling herbs such as basil amid your rows of vegetables. Bees find both irresistible.

A CRICKET IN THE HOUSE IS GOOD LUCK

How True Is It?
Only if you consider insect infestations good fortune.

In almost every part of the world a cricket in the house is considered good luck. In China, a whole "cricket culture" developed some 2000 years ago. The appeal of the cricket to the Chinese went beyond its charming "song." The Chinese valued large families with many children. Since crickets lay hundreds of eggs, they were considered models of fruitfulness and prosperity. In some parts of China, it was traditional to wish newlyweds as many children as a cricket.

During the Tang Dynasty (500 B.C.-618 A.D.) it became the custom among the Chinese to keep a cricket in a beautifully constructed box or cage so they could carry the cricket with them and enjoy its music wherever they went. This custom spread to Japan and even to Europe.

Unlike other varieties such as locusts which devour crops and mole crickets which ruin plants and lawns by chewing through the roots, the house cricket (its scientific name is *Gryllidae*) is harmless. And unlike the ladybug, which feeds on insects humans regard as pests, the cricket is a vegetarian. It has no practical purpose. With one exception.

By its chirps, the snowy tree cricket (*Oecanthus niveus*) can actually tell you how cold it is outside. Here's the formula:

Count the number of chirps per minute.

Subtract 40.

Divide this number by 4.

Add 50, and you'll have the outdoor temperature in Fahrenheit.

True, it seems odd, but it actually works. Because crickets are sensitive to changes in air temperature, they chirp more slowly as the outdoor temperature drops, or faster as the outdoor temperature rises.

IT'S BAD LUCK TO KILL A SPIDER

How True Is It?
Sorry, Miss Muffet, but they're nicer to have around than you think.

There are somewhere in the neighborhood of 35,000 species of spiders, and almost without exception they are nasty, aggressive, predatory, cannibalistic little beasts that will kill and eat anything that makes the mistake of wandering into their territory. That includes members of the spider's own immediate family. Clearly, then, we can only do good by squashing spiders wherever we find them, and the old wives' tale that encourages us to make nice with these eight-legged pests is way off the mark. Right?

Well, actually, no. Spiders that live in the corners of a house prey on many of the insects that make us humans miserable—most notably mosquitoes and cockroaches. Furthermore, science is discovering new uses for spider silk.

Most spiders spin a line of silk as they move about, just in case they have to make a sudden drop to escape a predator (just like Spiderman). The smaller species of spiders migrate by spinning a long strand of silk and then letting air currents carry it to a new habitat. Female spiders often create a silk sac in which to carry their eggs. Spiders that live underground close off the entrance to their burrow with a silk trap door. And some male spiders use their silk to tie up a female during the mating season. The spiders aren't getting kinky: female spiders are often larger than the males, and the lady spider in question may decide she would prefer the male courting her as a meal instead of a mate.

All of these varied uses for spider silk, not to mention its strength and resiliency, have intrigued scientists. At the University of Wyoming at Laramie a team of researchers led by Professor Randy Lewis has succeeded in discovering the formula by which spiders convert liquid proteins into silk. Dr. Lewis and his team are trying to create a synthetic spider silk that is stronger and more flexible than spiders produce.

One possibility for synthetic spider silk is body armor. The plastic known as Kevlar which is used today for body armor is extremely strong, "but it's not very stretchy," as Todd Blackledge, an entomologist at the University of Akron, puts it. The researchers are hoping to develop a body armor that feels and fits more like Lycra.

But synthetic spider silk could have many other uses as well, especially in medicine, where the extremely thin silk could be used to make extremely thin sutures for eye or nerve surgery.

Another unexpected possibility for synthetic spider silk is air bags. "Right now an air bag just sort of blasts you back into a seat," said Dr. Lewis. "But if it were made out of this material it would actually be made to absorb energy and really reduce impact."

The researchers still have a long way to go. At this stage synthetic spider silk doesn't replicate the strength of real spider silk, and the synthetic threads are too thick. But researchers such as Dr. Blackledge and Dr. Lewis are confident that in time they will get the formula right.

Section Nine

Chicken Soup Is a Great Cold and Flu Remedy, and Other Old Wives' Tales About Food

HELP FIGHT
COLDS!

CHICKEN SOUP IS A GREAT COLD AND FLU REMEDY

How True Is It?
It's not good for the chicken, but it's great for you.

Generations have been nursed through colds and flu with a steaming bowl of chicken soup. The remedy is so strongly associated with Jewish grandmothers that chicken soup has been nicknamed "Jewish penicillin." In fact, it was a Jewish philosopher and physician, Moses Maimonides, who back in the 12th century first recommended chicken soup for cold and flu sufferers.

But is there anything to this long-standing tradition? You bet there is. Scientific literature across the globe agrees that chicken soup is packed with good stuff. As it simmers, chicken releases into the broth the amino acid cysteine which, just like the drug acetylcysteine prescribed for bronchitis and other respiratory ailments, reduces the build-up of mucus and helps you breathe easier.

A study by the National University of Singapore went a step farther. It found that chicken soup is not only good for colds, but it is also good for a healthy heart. When laboratory rats that had been bred to develop high blood pressure were fed mass-produced, over-the-counter chicken stock (not even homemade!), researchers found that, over the course of a year, the rats' heart swelling was reduced by 40% to 50%, and the thickening of their blood vessels was reduced by 60%.

The Singapore scientists believe the secret ingredient is a type of protein known as a peptide. Just about all meat contains peptides, yet only peptide from chickens made human blood vessels healthier. Peptides from other meats, such as pork or

Dr. Rennard's List of the Top 5 Most Effective Commercial Chicken Soups

1. Knorr's Chicken Flavor Chicken Noodle
2. Campbell's Home Cookin' Chicken Vegetable
3. Campbell's Healthy Request Chicken Noodle
4. Lipton Cup-O-Soup, Chicken Noodle
5. Progresso Chicken Noodle

beef, were also tested, but they had no effect. The researchers still are not sure why chicken peptide works when others do not.

One of the most interesting studies of the chicken soup phenomenon was conducted by Stephen Rennard, M.D., chief of pulmonary medicine at the University of Nebraska Medical Center in Omaha. He tested the chicken soup recipe handed down to his wife from her Lithuanian grandmother. Dr. Rennard found that chicken soup has anti-inflammatory properties. Coughing and congestion, two common symptoms of colds and flu, are the result of inflammation produced by white blood cells known as neutrophils that pile up in the bronchial tubes. In the lab Dr. Rennard found that chicken soup diminished the ability of neutrophils to accumulate. Chicken soup proved so potent that even when it had been diluted 200 times it was still a good neutrophil inhibitor.

And there's more: although Dr. Rennard's grandmother-in-law's recipe does not call for it, you can boost your chicken soup's antiviral and antibacterial properties by adding garlic. And don't leave out the pepper—it contains capsaicin which works like cough medicine, suppressing coughs and reducing mucus. Even the heat of the soup helps loosen congestion, while the broth helps to keep you hydrated—absolutely essential for all cold and flu sufferers.

Grandma's Chicken Soup

from Dr. Rennard

1 five-to-six-lb stewing hen or baking chicken	2 turnips
1 package of chicken wings	1 to 2 large carrots
3 large onions	5 to 6 celery stems
1 large sweet potato	1 bunch of parsley
3 parsnips	1 clove garlic diced
	Salt and pepper to taste

Clean the whole chicken, put it in a large pot, and cover it with cold water. Bring the water to a boil. Add the chicken wings, onions, sweet potato, parsnips, turnips and carrots. Boil about 1.5 hours. Remove fat from the surface as it accumulates. Add the parsley, celery and garlic. Cook the mixture about 45 minutes longer. Remove the chicken and chicken wings. The chicken is not used further for the soup. (The meat makes excellent chicken parmesan.) Put the vegetables in a food processor until they are chopped fine or pass through the strainer and then return them to the soup. Both methods were performed in the present study. Salt and pepper to taste. (Note: this soup freezes well.)

Of course, some cold sufferers have no talent in the kitchen. For them, Dr. Rennard also tested commercial chicken soup and found still more good news: canned chicken soup is just as effective as homemade. Although it doesn't taste as good as Grandma's.

CHINESE GINGER AND SPRING ONION SOUP IS A GREAT COLD AND FLU REMEDY

How True Is It?
Stick with the chicken soup.

Feed a cold, starve a fever, is what old wives say in the West. But in China, starve a cold/starve a fever is the rule. Traditional Chinese healers argue that rich, nutritious foods will only strengthen the cold or flu and make it linger longer. Consequently, giving sick people a bowl of chicken soup is out of the question.

A classic Chinese cold and flu remedy is a soup made with ginger and the white part of a spring onion. The most important ingredient is the ginger which is said to eliminate chills, reduce cough and congestion, and soothe headache and aching muscles. According to traditional Chinese medicine, ginger's hot, spicy quality generates sweat, thus pushing the virus out through the patient's pores. To meet the demand, both in the sickroom and in the kitchen, 2 million pounds of ginger are produced in Asia annually. But alas, there is no scientific data to support the supposed benefits of ginger for fighting a cold.

Ginger is good, however, for an upset stomach. Two tablespoons of thinly sliced fresh ginger root steeped for several minutes in a mug of boiling water will soothe the nausea that often accompanies flu or a bad cold. It also works well for stomach cramps, the queasiness associated with motion sickness and pregnancy, and indigestion.

WINE IS GOOD FOR YOU

How True Is It?
True—as long as you're only drinking a glass or two a day.

Two thousand years ago St. Timothy, a disciple of St. Paul, suffered from chronic stomach trouble. In a letter to his young friend the great apostle broke off his instructions on how to run a church to offer a little medical advice. "Take a little wine," St. Paul wrote, "for thy stomach's sake."

More recently there have been reports that the French and Italians have a lower level of cholesterol and suffer less from heart disease than their American cousins—this in spite of a diet that is rich in cream, butter, and cheese—because every day they drink red wine.

Other health benefits have been attributed to the fruit of the grape, but is there any scientific data to back it up? Happily, the answer is yes.

Researchers at Chicago's Northwestern University Medical School found that the stuff that does the trick is resveratrol, a form of estrogen that is concentrated in grape skins that produce red wine. Out in the vineyard nature created resveratrol to protect grapes against fungal infections. In the lab, however, researchers have discovered that resveratrol also acts as an antioxidant and an anticoagulant. It also has been found to be toxic to prostate cancer cells, while leaving healthy cells unharmed.

Meanwhile, in Spain, researchers at the Spanish Council for Scientific Research reported that if grapes are subjected to low levels of ultraviolet irradiation before they are made into wine, the level of resveratrol will increase from one milligram in a glass of red wine to more than three milligrams. In other words, a little ultraviolet irradiation is all it takes to deliver three times the health benefits in each glass of red wine.

But what if you prefer white wine? After all, the resveratrol-packed grape skins are removed from the vats in order to make white wine. No problem. Scientists in Israel have discovered a method to increase the level of resveratrol in white wine. By fermenting the whole squeezed grapes in alcohol for 18 hours before removing their skins, the antioxidants in the white wine were increased six times above their normal level. This method also boosted the amount of sugar in the white wine, creating something akin to a sweet dessert wine.

But wine is not just good for the body, it is also good for the brain, especially for those in the more creative professions. Six thousand British government employees were recruited for a study sponsored by the University of London. In a series of tests that measured memory, general intelligence, and mathematical and verbal skills, teetotalers scored lowest. Those who drank one alcoholic beverage a week did a bit better, while those who drank a half bottle of wine every day had the highest test scores. Researchers found that the alcohol fired up the brain cells and made the wine drinker more imaginative and more productive.

Good news aside, because of the well-established detrimental effects of excessive alcohol consumption on the body, the old wives—and doctors—advise everyone to drink in moderation.

AN APPLE A DAY KEEPS THE DOCTOR AWAY

How True Is It?
Your HMO will be thrilled: apples have tremendous health benefits.

Among all the varieties of fruits, the apple is so simple, so ordinary, so ubiquitous that it may seem hard to swallow the claim that a mere apple a day will keep the doctor away. Nonetheless, plenty of medical evidence from around the world backs up what old wives have been saying for generations. In fact, you can derive a host of health benefits simply by drinking apple cider or apple juice.

Researchers at the agricultural school of Hirosaki University, located in the heart of Japan's Apple Belt, found that juice made from small, immature apples—the ones apple farmers routinely throw away—are packed with antioxidants known as polyphenols—up to 10 times the amount of polyphenols found in fully ripe apples. These polyphenols encourage the production of natural-killer (NK) cells which target cancer cells.

That's great news. But apples can do much more. For example, the juice in apples interacts with gastric juices in the stomach to reduce intestinal disorders. The sugar in apples does not raise a body's blood sugar level, which means the fruit is effective in preventing diabetes. (This is true of the sugar in virtually all fruits.) Apples can prevent heart disease by reducing the level of bad cholesterol and boosting the body's good cholesterol. And when you feel rundown, reach for an apple: the citric acid in apples can help the body recover from fatigue.

And there's more good news. Dr. Chang Y. Cy Lee, a professor of food science at Cornell University in New York, reports that apples contain a chemical compound known as quercetin that can protect brain cells from the damage caused by such diseases as Alzheimer's and Parkinson's. A preliminary study from the Mayo Clinic in Rochester, Minnesota, suggests that quercetin also may block the male hormones that encourage the growth of prostate cancer cells. And researchers at London's Kings College and University of Southampton in England are studying evidence that suggests quercetin can reduce the risk of contracting lung diseases such as asthma, bronchitis and emphysema.

FISH IS BRAIN FOOD

How True Is It?
Nothing fishy here—it's true.

Bertie Wooster, the barely averagely astute hero of countless Jeeves-and-Wooster stories by P.G. Wodehouse, always believed that his valet Jeeves must have consumed fish by the barrelful. What else could account for Jeeves' prodigious ability to get Bertie and his feckless pals out of one fearsome scrape after another?

It turns out that on the subject of seafood's ability to stimulate the little gray cells, Bertie was right on the money. Scientists suspected as much back in the 19th century, although those early proponents of the fish-is-brain-food school of nutrition mistakenly believed it was the phosphorus in fish that did the job. Today, researchers believe a fatty compound known as docosahexaenoic acid (DHA) is the stuff that makes the brain work harder and better. In fact, DHA is the fundamental building block of brain tissue. The more DHA the body takes in through diet, the more fuel the brain has to work with. On the other hand, a diet low in DHA could translate into deficient brain function.

Some medical studies have found evidence that people who eat a lot of seafood (and consequently have high levels of DHA) are less susceptible to depression. A report published in the *American Journal of Clinical Nutrition* found that in fish-eating nations such as Japan and Korea the incidence of depression among the populace is low. At the opposite end of the spectrum are nations such as the United States and Canada where fish is eaten rarely, DHA levels are low, and depression rates are high.

In a separate study researchers in The Netherlands found that elderly men who ate a lot of fish were less likely than their meat-eating neighbors to suffer from memory loss. Meanwhile, in Japan, researchers reported improved short-term memory among patients who received DHA supplements.

The University of Texas Medical Branch in Galveston studied the impact of fish on memory from a different angle. High levels of zinc are found in fish. The Texas team found that memory as well as other basic brain functions decline in individuals whose diet does not include much zinc. When participants in the Texas study started eating higher levels of zinc-rich foods, such as fish, their verbal recall skills increased 12 percent and their ability to remember visual patterns jumped 17 percent.

Researchers at England's University of Surrey teamed up with their colleagues at Purdue University in Indiana and discovered links between low levels of DHA and such disorders as dyslexia, attention deficit disorder, and hyperactivity.

After studying DHA levels in children, Professor Michael Crawford, director of London's Institute of Brain Chemistry and Human Nutrition, reported that schoolkids with the highest levels of DHA behaved better and outperformed their classmates who showed low levels of DHA. Professor Crawford has gone on the record to encourage pregnant women to eat a lot of fish such as salmon, pollock and shrimp, arguing that the brainiac benefits of DHA in the mother's body will be passed along to her unborn child.

Coldwater fish, particularly salmon, tuna, mackerel, and herring, have the highest levels of DHA. All it takes is a couple seafood meals a week to boost your DHA level and do your brain some good.

A word of caution: pregnant women should avoid certain types of fish that tend to have high levels of mercury. These fish include tuna, mackerel, shark, swordfish, snapper, orange roughy, marlin, and grouper.

CARROTS ARE GOOD FOR THE EYES

How True Is It?
If they could afford them, some rabbits might need glasses.

Some old wives believe that eating carrots is good for your eyesight in general. Other old wives insist that eating carrots provides a very specific benefit—namely, improved night vision.

Alas, both teams of old wives are a bit off the mark. Carrots do not sharpen your eyesight or boost your night vision. Carrots may, however, prevent macular degeneration, an eye disease that eventually leads to blindness. The secret ingredient is betacarotene that is present in spades in carrots (as well as in other vegetables such as squash, cabbage, spinach, and dandelion greens). In 1988 researchers at the University of Chicago studied 3,000 elderly Americans and found that something so simple as eating a single carrot a day reduced the risk of macular degeneration by as much as 40 percent.

Neil Bressler of the Johns Hopkins Medical Institutions in Baltimore, Maryland, came to the same conclusion regarding the positive effects of betacarotene. But Bressler found that for prevention of macular degeneration, betacarotene should be part of a vitamin-supplements program that includes vitamins C, E, zinc, and zinc oxide, all of which work to keep eyes healthy.

CHILDREN SHOULDN'T DRINK COFFEE AS IT WILL STUNT THEIR GROWTH

How True Is It?
There's some truth here—but most kids don't like coffee anyway!

Concerned grandparents who would never dream of giving their grandchildren coffee because it will stunt the kids' growth will cheerfully pass around cans of soft drinks. There is a factual disconnect going on here, because the coffee and virtually all soft drinks are top-heavy with caffeine.

A high intake of caffeine does cause the body to lose the calcium and potassium it needs in order for bone to grow. One study found that caffeine decreases bone-mineral density in teenage girls. The same study concluded, however, that the ill-effects of caffeine can be offset by drinking just one glass of milk per day. In other words, unless the kid is knocking back double shots of espresso all day long, there's not much to worry about.

Dr. Manfred Kroger, professor of food science at Pennsylvania State University, has explained that caffeine is more of an issue for kids than for adults because a child's body is smaller and it tends to retain caffeine in its system longer than is the case with adults. Consequently, Dr. Kroger recommends that kids consume no more than 100 mg of caffeine a day. That translates to about two cans of soda, one shot of espresso, or one foamy specialty coffee drink.

When it comes to caffeine, not all soft drinks are packing the samc wallop. Root beer has virtually no caffeine. Most clear soft drinks are caffeine-free—but not all of them. Interestingly, citrus soft drinks tend to have 20 percent more caffeine than colas. Obviously, a concerned parent must start reading soft-drink can labels.

And here is something else to worry about: often when kids get thirsty, their first impulse is to grab a soft drink. Because of the diuretic effects of caffeine in the soft drink, however, the kids are actually becoming more dehydrated than they were already. Young athletes in particular should steer away from soft drinks to quench their thirst: their best bet is to drink water or fruit or vegetable juices.

BOYS WHO DRINK COFFEE WILL BE BEARDLESS

How True Is It?
Only if they shave.

Old wives in Turkey fear that young boys who drink coffee will never be able to grow a beard. Could there really be a link between caffeine and testosterone? Professor Peter Elsner and his team at Jena University in Germany found that there is indeed a link between caffeine and testosterone—but not in the way that Turkish old wives fear. Caffeine products, the Jena University researchers said, can actually stop men from going bald.

Guys with high testosterone levels tend to have a lot of body and facial hair. It's a matter of genetics. Some families have buckets of the 5-alpha reductase enzyme, the stuff that encourages testosterone to produce a heavy beard and jungle of hair on a guy's chest, belly, and back.

There is a downside to all this masculinity: what the 5-alpha reductase enzyme giveth, the 5-alpha reductase enzyme also taketh away. Or to put it in plain English, hairy-chested he-men tend to go bald.

The trick to stimulating hair growth is not drinking coffee—you'd have to drink 60 to 80 cups per day before there was enough caffeine in your system to actually reach the roots of your hair. Nor will rubbing coffee grounds on your scalp do any good. Instead, you must rub the caffeine extract right on the place where you want the hair to grow. Professor Elsner's study found that the caffeine treatment, on average, increased hair growth by 46 percent and extended the life cycle of the hair by 37 percent.

If baldness runs in your family, Professor Elsner suggests that you take pre-emptive action by starting to massage a caffeine solution into your scalp now so your hair won't fall out later.

POTATOES WITH A GREENISH TINGE ARE POISONOUS

How True Is It?
True, but when it comes to poison content, we're talking small potatoes.

Back in the 16th century, when the white potato first found its way from South America to Europe, it was not immediately popular. In England, Queen Elizabeth I's cook threw out the potato, cooked the greens of the potato vine, and served them to Her Majesty. Elizabeth did not like the result. Still, the potato hung around in England, although only as an ornamental plant in English gardens.

While the English wrote off the potato as unpalatable, it developed a much worse reputation in other parts of the globe. French farmers believed eating a potato would cause leprosy. And colonists in America thought white potatoes were poisonous. These old suspicions regarding the nutritious, delicious potato may be the source for the old wives' tale that potatoes that show a touch a green under their skin are toxic.

Potatoes, of course, grow underground and are happiest when they remain in the dark. These days potatoes move from the field to the supermarket, where they spend days under the glare of artificial light. It is the constant exposure to light that produces the greenish color under the potato's skin.

This green color is solanine. Yes, solanine is toxic, but according to *Science Daily*, you would have to ingest 200 milligrams of solanine in order to give yourself a lethal dose of green-potato poison. Although a completely green potato could be packing 200 milligrams of solanine, it is unlikely that anyone would choose to eat it.

Generally the green tint is limited to the potato skin. Simply cut it off and cook the potato as you usually would.

Fun Facts About Potatoes

- Archaeological evidence tells us that the Incas of Peru were cultivating potatoes by 200 B.C.
- The potato came to Europe via the Spanish conquistadores who encountered it in the Andes of South America in 1537.
- The average American eats about 140 pounds of potatoes, and the average European consumes about 280 pounds of potatoes per year.
- The record for peeling the most potatoes using standard kitchen knives was set on March 17, 1981, at the Bourke Street Hall in Melbourne, Australia. The winners—J. Mills, M. McDonald, P. Jennings, E. Dardiner, and V. McNulty—peeled 266.5 kg or 587 lbs., 8 oz. of potatoes in 45 minutes.

COOL FOODS ARE GOOD FOR A FEVER

How True Is It?
Don't let them feed you this line.

In India, indeed in many parts of Asia, food tends to be divided into two large groups: cool and hot, and each of these types of food are appropriate for different circumstances. During the sultry Asian summer, for example, Ng Siong Mui, the author of *Secrets of Nutritional Chinese Cookery*, suggests that you will be able to endure the heat and humidity better if you stay away from hot foods such as curry, red meat, anything fried, and chocolate. In place of beverages that stir up the blood, such as alcohol, you should drink chilled lime juice or iced lemon tea.

According to traditional Indian medicine, anyone suffering from a fever also should be fed only cool foods such as light soups, fish, yogurt drinks, and fruit. But will eating food that is cool or chilled actually diminish a fever? Yes, but only up to a point.

According to the doctors at North Shore General Pediatrics in New York, "Fever is the body's normal response to infections and helps to fight them off by turning on the body's immune system." The doctors explain that a fever is not an illness in itself, rather it is a symptom of an illness. There are ways to alleviate the symptom so the patient is more comfortable, but the fever won't go away entirely until the illness has been cured.

Eating cool foods may make the patient feel a bit better. And if you take the patient's temperature using an oral thermometer right after he or she has downed a bowl of chilled tomato soup, you will get a reading that shows the fever has dropped. But it is a false reading. The chilled soup has lowered the body temperature a bit, but only temporarily; it has done nothing to cure the underlying illness. Come back 30 minutes later and take the patient's temperature again and you'll find that the fever is back up to its pre-cool-food level.

By all means, serve cool foods to the sick person. It will make him or her feel better temporarily. But don't expect cool food to affect a cure. The immune system will do that by itself.

IT'S DANGEROUS TO EAT OYSTERS IN MONTHS THAT DO NOT HAVE AN "R" IN THEM

How True Is It?
Or so the oysters would have us believe ...

The English have always been wild about oysters. Even Englishmen who lived miles away from the coast managed to get their hands on the tasty bivalves, as witnessed by the huge deposits of oyster shells archaeologists have uncovered in 2000-year-old dumps along Hadrian's Wall on the English-Scotch border.

Wherever the English went they took their preference for oysters with them. The Pilgrims in Massachusetts were delighted to find immense oyster beds just steps away from their cabins. But the English also carried with them this bit of oyster lore: only eat oysters during months that have an "r" in them; anyone who slurps down an oyster during May, June, July, or August is just asking for trouble.

There is something to this. For all those centuries before refrigeration, shellfish spoiled quickly during the summer months. And there was another reason to leave oysters alone during the summer: it is the period when oysters spawn.

According to the proprietors of the Golden Point Oyster Sea Farm in Maine, spawning takes a lot out of the oyster, leaving the meat tasting "watery, runny, lacking flavor, and generally not worth eating." It's best to wait "until they recover a bit by feeding for a month or two." In other words, wait until September—an "r" month.

Today, of course, refrigeration is not a concern. And oysters can be overnighted from their beds to virtually anywhere in the world. The only reason then not to eat oysters during the summer months is a matter of taste.

YOU BURN MORE CALORIES EATING A STICK OF CELERY THAN ARE CONTAINED IN THE CELERY STICK

How True Is It?
Stick to the facts—this one's false.

Negative-calorie foods are the Holy Grail of dieters. Imagine a food that has so few calories that you burn up more just in the act of chewing and digesting it! Alas, imaginary is the right word for such a notion.

True, celery is very low in calories—there are about six calories in an eight-inch celery stalk. But by eating celery you are not kicking your body's calorie burner into overdrive. The Health and Fitness News Service reports that eating celery "burns only about the same number of calories as sitting and staring into space." This applies to the other miracle "negative calorie" food, green bell peppers, and the fad diet of the mid-1990s, cabbage soup.

So that's the downside of celery.

On the upside, celery is a good source of fiber. It is inexpensive and available in the supermarket all-year-round. And four ounces of raw celery—about three stalks—is rich in vitamin C and is a good source of potassium.

But the bottom line is, if you want to lose weight, you have to reduce your intake of calories, or find activities that will burn off more calories. The myth about negative-calorie foods is, according to Kelly Brownell, director of the Yale University Center for Eating Disorders, "just another sign of people looking for magic in weight loss."

WHITE SPOTS ON YOUR FINGERNAILS MEAN YOU NEED CALCIUM

How True Is It?
It's more likely you're clumsy.

The old wives are right in one respect: fingernails do offer clues about health problems, but low calcium is not one of them. According to food folklore, white spots on the fingernails mean that your diet is deficient in calcium, and a few glasses of milk will clear up the problem.

In fact those white spots are a sign that the nail has suffered some kind of minor injury, such as a bump or a bruise. It's not serious, and the white spots will disappear as the nail grows out.

But keep an eye on your fingernails for telltale signs of more serious trouble. Dr. Louise Martin, a dermatologist at Providence Hospital in Rhode Island, explains how to recognize what your fingernails are telling you. Brittle or slow-growing nails are a sign that the nails are dehydrated, a common complaint among people who wear artificial nails or who spend a lot of time in water, such as swimmers. The solution in this case is to apply a heavy moisturizer such as petroleum jelly at night before going to bed. (And wear cotton gloves so the petroleum jelly doesn't smear all over your bedding.)

A dark brown or black streak on one fingernail could be a sign of cancer. Nails with a bluish tinge may be a sign of lung trouble. Nails that are turning yellow may indicate liver problems. In addition to color, the shape of the nails offers clues. Club nails, or nails which curl down around the tip of your fingers, can be a warning sign of lung or heart disease. Little dimples in your nails may be the result of a skin condition such as psoriasis.

But don't try to self-diagnose yourself based on the appearance of your fingernails. If you notice something out of the ordinary happening to your nails, go to a doctor.

FLAT GINGER ALE IS GOOD FOR A QUEASY STOMACH

How True Is It?
This one's based on fizzy logic.

In January 1988 the late President Ronald Reagan was looking forward to a luncheon visit with Japanese Prime Minister Noboru Takeshita when he was struck down by a stomach virus. By the time the Japanese Prime Minister arrived at the White House, Reagan was feeling well enough to greet his guest and join him for lunch. But while Takeshita dined on salmon bisque and breast of Cornish game hen, Reagan limited himself to consommé and flat ginger ale.

Ginger is thought to soothe a queasy stomach, but Dr. Don McConnell, an emergency pediatrician at Edmonton's University Hospital, has found that "most ginger ale has so little ginger it's not effective and the sugar in the pop makes diarrhea worse." Dr. Dianne Brox of the Alberta Medical Association agrees and suggests electrolyte drinks for kids and sport drinks or unsweetened herbal tea for nauseated teens and adults.

With stomach viruses the dehydration brought on by bouts of vomiting or diarrhea is the greatest worry. Young children and the elderly are especially susceptible to dehydration, and as noted above the sugar in ginger ale or other soft drinks only contributes to the problem. To restore the salts and minerals the ailing body needs at this time, sports drinks that replace electrolytes are the best.

IT'S SAFE TO EAT FOOD DROPPED ON THE FLOOR IF YOU PICK IT UP WITHIN FIVE SECONDS

How True Is It?
Five-second rules are made to be broken.

It's known across the land as the "Five-Second Rule." Any kind of food that hits the floor or the ground is still safe to eat—provided you pick it up within five seconds.

If the Five-Second Rule sounds totally arbitrary, that's because it is.

During an internship at Professor Hans Blaschek's lab at the University of Illinois during the summer of 2003, Jillian Clarke, an enterprising and uber-smart 16-year-old student at the Chicago High School for Agricultural Sciences, conducted a series of experiments to test the veracity of the Five-Second Rule. She dropped Gummi Bears and fudge cookies on ceramic tiles upon which she had brushed E. coli, a type of bacteria found in raw meat and human feces, and one which we run into just about everywhere everyday.

After she had dropped the Gummi Bears and the fudge cookies on the infected tiles, she studied them under an electron microscope. Clarke found that E. coli stuck to the candy and the cookies even if she snatched them up within the five-second window of opportunity.

But there's more. Clarke did a demographic study of the Five-Second Rule and discovered that:

1. 70 percent of women and 56 percent of men follow the 5-Second Rule.
2. People are more likely to pick up and eat cookies and candy. If the dropped food is a vegetable such as cauliflower or broccoli, they don't exercise the Five-Second Rule.

Section Ten

A Severed Head Stays Alive for Several Minutes, and Other Old Wives' Tales About the Life of Crime

A SEVERED HEAD STAYS ALIVE FOR SEVERAL MINUTES AFTER IT'S BEEN SEPARATED FROM THE BODY

How True Is It?
Well ...

Mechanical head-chopping devices have been around at least since 1307,when a beheading machine was set up near the town of Meron, Ireland, to execute a scalawag named Murcod Ballagh. But the Cuisinart of head removers was the guillotine, named for Doctor Antoine Louis Guillotine, who designed the sleek, efficient gadget that decapitated King Louis XVI, Queen Marie Antoinette, and thousands of less distinguished victims during the French Revolution's Reign of Terror.

Although the guillotine is almost universally regarded with

> When the guillotine made its debut at the Place de Grève on April 25, 1792, for the execution of Nicolas-Jacques Pelletier, a robber who brutalized his victim, the assembled crowd was underwhelmed. After the execution the mob called for the return of the gallows on which it took the condemned much longer to die and therefore put on a much better show. But soon the mob became attached to the guillotine, if for no other reason that it could dispatch more victims in a single day than any other method available in the late 18th century. (In Lyon, on a single day in December 1793, the guillotine took the lives of 209 victims).

horror these days, Dr. Guillotine intended it as a swift, tidy, and humane form of execution. He and the leaders of the Revolution were determined to have a mode of capital punishment in keeping with the principles of the Age of Enlightenment. Compared to the unspeakable agonies of being burned alive at the stake, or having one's bones smashed while bound to a wheel, the guillotine was a genuinely merciful step forward. Dr. Guillotine himself described his device as "philanthropic."

Soon after the guillotine was in regular operation, executioners and others on the scaffold began to notice that the severed heads often seemed to still be "alive." The eyes opened or twitched. The lips trembled, or the mouth opened as if the victim were trying to speak.

The most famous case is that of Charlotte Corday, the young woman who stabbed to death the French revolutionary Murat while he soaked in his bath tub. After she was guillotined, the executioner lifted her head out of the basket and displayed it to the crowd as he slapped its face. Corday's cheeks reddened and her face took on an angry expression. The old wives said that the guillotine worked so swiftly that for several minutes after the head was separated from the body it remained alive and conscious. The idea was terribly unsettling, to say the least.

This notion hung on so long that in 1905 a French physician named Beaurieux decided to settle the matter by studying the head of a criminal named Languille who was scheduled to be guillotined at 5:30 a.m. on June 28, 1905.

After the blade of the guillotine fell, Dr. Beaurieux observed, "The eyelids and lips of the guillotined man worked in irregularly rhythmic contractions for about five or six seconds." Beaurieux waited a few seconds more until he saw the muscles of the face relax and the eyelids half close.

Then he says, "I called in a strong, sharp voice, 'Languille!'

I saw the eyelids slowly lift up, without any spasmodic contractions—I insist advisedly on this peculiarity—but with an even movement, quite distinct and normal, such as happens in everyday life, with people awakened or torn from their thoughts.... Languille's eyes very definitely fixed themselves on mine and the pupils focused themselves. I was not, then, dealing with the sort of vague dull look without any expression, that can be observed any day in dying people to whom one speaks: I was dealing with undeniably living eyes which were looking at me."

After several seconds, the eyelids closed again. Once again the doctor called out the "dead" man's name. "Once more, without any spasm, slowly, the eyelids lifted and undeniably living eyes fixed themselves on mine with perhaps even more penetration than the first time."

The eyelids closed again, and when Beaurieux called Languille's name for the third time there was no reaction. He lifted the lids with his fingers and recognized that the eyes had taken on "the glazed look which they have in death."

According to Dr. Beaurieux, the whole scene took about 25 to 30 seconds.

Languille may have remained conscious for a few seconds after being beheaded. However, his remaining conscious for 25 to 30 seconds seems unlikely. When the head is severed from the body, both parts quickly lose enormous amounts of blood. Blood loss leads—in rapid succession—to a massive drop in blood pressure, oxygen deprivation (cerebral hypoxia, as doctors call it), unconsciousness, and brain death.

IT'S BAD LUCK TO BUY A HOUSE WHERE A MURDER TOOK PLACE

How True Is It?
Not at all.

The toughest job for a real estate agent is trying to sell a house that was the scene of a murder or some other violent crime. Potential buyers regard the room where the death took place as haunted—a conviction no amount of sales spin can overcome. If the tragedy occurred outside the house, the realtor's job is a bit easier, but there is still a nasty stigma attached to the property. The headache, then, is not trying to get imaginary ghosts out of the house, but trying to get new tenants in.

The Benedict Canyon bungalow where actress Sharon Tate and her friends were massacred by Charles Manson's "family" had to be knocked down—no buyer would touch it.

The horrific reputation of the murderer/cannibal Jeffrey Dahmer not only had an impact on the apartment building where he lived, but upon his entire Milwaukee neighborhood. Occupancy on Dahmer's old street fell from 80 percent to 20 percent. People just did not want to live anywhere near such an awful crime scene. The neighborhood did not begin to stabilize again until an urban redevelopment company bought the building where Dahmer had lived, and then leveled it.

The $4 million house where Eric and Lyle Menendez killed their parents sat on the market for two years before the realtor found a buyer. And even then the house sold for a fraction of its previous value.

The chic condominium where Nicole Brown Simpson and Ron Goldman were murdered also sat on the market for over two years before it found a buyer. The highly desirable Brentwood address, the 3400-square-feet of living space, the four bedrooms, three bathrooms, and rooftop patio—none of these could overcome the taint of the double murders. When the condo finally did sell, it was at a price far lower than one would expect for a comparable home in Brentwood.

Randall Bell of Bell & Associates in Laguna Niguel, California, has made appraising and selling stigmatized properties his specialty. He says that real estate agents should expect to discount houses that were a notorious crime scene by as much as 25 percent. In time, Bell says, the stigma goes away, "but it takes 10 to 25 years."

In other words, houses where murders have taken place mean less money for real-estate agents and homeowners. But those in the market for a house may be passing up a real bargain if they let superstition get in the way of common sense and scientific evidence.

Ghosts and Satan, as *The Skeptic's Dictionary* points out, could change addresses any time if they truly had the powers old wives' tales say they do. So why would they stay in one place for centuries, particularly one where bad things happened to them?

Older homes provide especially fertile ground for so-called paranormal activity. But eerie sounds occur, in part, when air passes through walls-even in a new building. Cracks and crevices, normal signs of wear and tear (or of bad builders) make room for drafts to seep in, not ghosts. And ghostbusting instruments designed to pick up the electromagnetic fields poltergeists allegedly give off work because of natural, not supernatural, phenomena. Most objects possess enough electromagnetic radiation to set the needles of these devices in motion.

Tips for Selling Crime Scene Houses

Real estate appraiser Randall Bell suggests three simple steps for getting a tainted property off the market.

1. Always tell a potential buyer that a crime took place in the house. Real estate agents can be taken to court if they fail to disclose such information.
2. Try to rent the house. Realize that immediately after the killing, no buyer will touch the place. But if you can get tenants into the house for a couple of years, that will go a long way toward diminishing its notoriety.
3. Renovate the property. Make it look different than it did on the day of the crime. Repaint. Change the appearance of the front door. Chop down existing trees, or plant new ones. Tear down an existing fence, or build a privacy wall. Remember that the house has been seen on television and cable news programs and in newspapers across the country (and possibly around the world). Make whatever changes necessary so it will not be instantly recognizable as "that house."

However, real-estate agents and homeowners saddled with stigmatized property can take a little comfort from knowing some people actually want to buy so-called haunted houses. Many like the prestige and excitement a ghostly inhabitant brings to their lives. And haunted-house tours can sometimes bring in a little extra money to help pay for the upkeep on an old house.

A DOG CAN SMELL BLOOD ON A MURDERER'S HANDS, EVEN YEARS AFTER THE CRIME

How True Is It?
The scent of blood does indeed linger, but not for years.

The image of baying bloodhounds chasing a runaway is burned into our collective memory—whether the scene comes out of Harriet Beecher Stowe's novel, *Uncle Tom's Cabin*, or the Coen Brothers comic film, *O Brother, Where Art Thou*. Although bloodhounds were bred originally to find game in the forest, as early as the 14th century they were being used to find fugitives. About the year 1305 the English used bloodhounds to track the Scottish patriot William Wallace, the renowned "Braveheart" of the Mel Gibson movie.

How can a dog pick up and follow a scent that no human can detect? Because a bloodhound's sense of smell is 1,000 times more powerful than a human's. We have about five million smelling cells in our nasal passages; dogs about 220 million. Bloodhounds are blessed not only with millions upon millions of olfactory cells by virtue of being dogs but also with especially long noses, wide nostrils, and heads designed for serious smelling. And this mysterious power lies at the root of the old wives' tale about a dog being able to smell human blood on the hands of killer, even years after the crime.

As often happens in old wives' tales, a scrap of truth is being blown way out of proportion. Bloodhounds can follow a cold trail, perhaps as long as five days after the person being hunted has passed that way. (Five days is a stretch even for the best tracking dog, and it assumes that there hasn't been rain or snow or some other event that would make detecting the trail impossible.) Within a few days of a violent crime a bloodhound can detect traces of blood no human can see on a rug or splattered on a wall. But expecting a bloodhound to pick up the scent of blood years after a murder is asking an awful lot of the pooch.

Today all types of dogs—not just bloodhounds—are trained by police, military, and search-and-rescue organizations to pick up the scent of survivors buried in the rubble of a building, or a person lost in an avalanche, or drugs or bombs hidden in a traveler's luggage.

BURGLARS CHECK THE NEWSPAPER OBITUARY PAGE TO SEE WHO'S DIED, THEN ROB THE HOUSE WHILE EVERYONE'S AT THE FUNERAL

How True Is It?
It's been known to happen.

Sometimes the old wives get it right. There really are professional thieves who target the homes of the recently deceased, cleaning out the place on the very day of the departed's funeral.

A notorious case occurred in 1996 in Pasadena, California, where two seemingly nice, polite sisters robbed the homes of at least 40 dead people.

The burglars, Helen Eposto, a 34-year-old nurse, and Jean Kolentik, a 32-year-old bookkeeper, had a system. In a black notebook they listed the names and addresses of who had died, who was away on vacation, or who was off on a honeymoon. In other words, they were getting their tips from the obituary page and the society column.

Although the police in Pasadena implicated the sisters in 40 residential burglaries, based on the enormous array of valuables they recovered, the cops were inclined to believe these women had robbed many more homes. "The loot," as Detective Ray Bartlett described it, filled an entire police storeroom. "And," he went on to say, "we've received calls from more than 300 persons who think they may have been victims of the sisters."

Some of the stuff found in the sisters' house astonished the cops. They couldn't imagine how two small women could have hauled away massive color televisions and heavy floor safes.

Pasadena is not the only city plagued by opportunistic burglars. In November 2003, police in Akron, Ohio, attributed at least three break-ins to obituary-reading thieves. The problem is sufficiently widespread in the state of Washington to lead its attorney-general's office to include the following caveat on its website in a bold-faced font:

> BEWARE:
> Some burglars will burglarize the homes of
> deceased persons at the time of the funeral service.
> Make arrangements to guard the home during funeral.

The sheriff's office in one Tennessee community offers to check its residents' homes during funerals—without charge. Numerous funeral homes provide instructions for bereaved families about practical matters such as death certificates; social security, veteran, and life insurance benefits; thank-you notes; cemetery markers-and thieves. And one security firm lists having a housesitter during funerals as a way to crimeproof a house.

The two sisters in Pasadena, though remarkably good at their jobs, are hardly alone. Thieves will turn your misfortune into good luck for themselves, so get a housesitter, call a neighbor, or notify your local police before you leave for your loved one's funeral.

IF THE HANGMAN'S ROPE BREAKS DURING AN EXECUTION, THE PRISONER IS INNOCENT

How True Is It?
Not very.

In earlier times the public execution of a criminal followed a pattern. The spectators lined the way to the gallows to see how the condemned carried himself (or herself), then crowded around the scaffold to hear the last words. After the execution of a particularly notorious lawbreaker, it was common for printers to capitalize on the occasion by churning out cheap pamphlets, complete with illustrations, that described the felon's last moments.

The spectators at a public hanging might differ as to the guilt of the condemned, but there was one point on which they all agreed: if the hangman's rope snapped, it was sign from God that the prisoner was innocent and he had to be set free.

Apparently no one argued that the rope was weak, or the condemned too heavy, or that the hangman somehow hadn't done his job properly. Divine intervention was the only explanation for a broken rope.

The roots of this old wives' tale go back at least 4000 years to a legal concept known as trial by ordeal. The idea is simple: God will not permit an innocent person to be punished and will intervene with a miracle to protect the innocent from harm.

The Romans, however, rejected as ridiculous the idea that a trial by ordeal would prove anything. But the barbarian tribes, especially in Germany, were big advocates of ordeals.

Ordeals took several forms. One was a duel, with the accused and the accuser fighting it out until one was dead. Another option called for red-hot irons. In this case the accused walked nine feet holding a red-hot iron in his hand, or walked barefoot over nine red-hot ploughshares. If his skin was not burned, he was considered innocent. A third popular option was the water ordeal. The accused was tied hand and foot and thrown into a pond or some other body of water. If he sank, he was considered guilty.

Even after the Germans converted to Christianity, the ordeal endured, in spite of frequent condemnations by the popes who objected strongly to the notion that one could strong-arm God into acting as referee in humankind's petty disputes. During the reign of Henry II, England stopped relying on ordeals except in cases where no other means for proving guilt or innocence were available, murders without witnesses or the alleged use of witchcraft, for example. In 1215, the Fourth Lateran Council ordered Catholic priests to stop using trials by ordeal. Adhering to this council's ruling, Henry III brought ordeals to a halt in England in 1220, replacing them with jury trials. By the Age of Enlightenment, the practice of ordeals had ended in Western Europe.

Anecdotal evidence, however, indicates trial by ordeal was not merely arbitrary. Notions of justice predate the modern era and many people survived trials by ordeal, often because a priest, probably noting that the evidence supported the innocence of the defendant or based on an assessment of the accused's character, intervened and determined the outcome of an ordeal. Ordeals, unlike our present legal system, appeared to begin with the assumption that a person was guilty until proven innocent, not vice versa.

Section Eleven

Chocolate Causes Acne, and Other Old Wives' Tales About the Human Body

CHOCOLATE CAUSES ACNE

How True Is It?
Chocoholics rejoice—it's not true.

As if high school weren't bad enough, that wretched period is when acne pops up on the face of virtually every teenager. It's Mother Nature's little joke: at the precise moment when kids are most self-conscious about their appearance, their faces become a minefield of pimples.

Trying to figure out how to make acne go away probably occupies as much of the adolescent mind as trying to figure out how to get a date. As we have seen, desperation is fertile ground for old wives' tales. The most widespread and persistent myth blames chocolate for bringing on acne. But that myth was exploded decades ago.

In 1969 medical researchers at the University of Pennsylvania School of Medicine recruited 65 volunteers who suffered from moderate acne. The doctors divided the subjects into two groups: one group ate candy bars packed with 10 times the usual amount of chocolate; the other group ate candy bars with no chocolate in them at all. At the end of four weeks, the volunteers who had eaten mega-amounts of chocolate showed no signs of increased acne.

So if it isn't chocolate, what does cause acne?

Acne flares up when the pores of the skin become blocked. Each pore is an opening to a follicle, a tiny canal with an oil gland. When everything is working normally, the oil gland flushes out the follicle, washing away old skin cells and keeping the skin moisturized. If the glands produce too much oil, the pores become blocked and produce a lump on the skin commonly called a pimple.

Infants have been known to have acne, and some people are still struggling with it in their 30s and 40s and beyond. But for most people, the curse comes upon them in adolescence. Blame it on hormones. With the onset of puberty, boys and girls produce a bumper crop of hormones called androgens. One of the things androgens do is cause the oil glands beneath the skin to enlarge and generate more oil. As we said earlier, excess oil tends to clog up the pores.

Other factors can make acne worse. Cosmetics, especially oil-based products, can block the pores. Drugs such as steroids, testosterone, and estrogen can cause acne. For young women, changes in the hormonal level leading up to the menstrual period can cause a flareup. Even genetics plays a role. Kids whose parents had bad bouts of acne will probably have the same trouble, too.

You can reduce acne to an extent by avoiding greasy makeup and oily skin lotions—using water-based products instead. And wash your face with a mild, non-abrasive soap. If the acne persists, a dermatologist can suggest a variety of treatments to clear it up. But giving up chocolate won't be one of them.

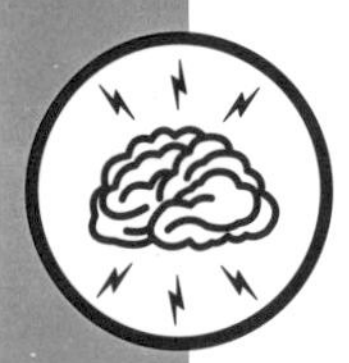

WE USE ONLY 10 PERCENT OF OUR BRAINS

How True Is It?
Think again.

If ever there was an old wives' tale with mass appeal, it is this one. Who could resist the notion that 90 percent of our brain is lying fallow, that we have the potential to leave Einstein in our intellectual dust?

If only it were true. Dr. Eric H. Chuder of the University of Washington's Department of Anesthesiology states, "I have not been able to track down the exact source of this myth, and I have never seen any scientific data to support it." Dr. Chuder is hardly alone. Barry L. Beyerstein of the Brain Behavior Laboratory at Simon Fraser University in Vancouver, Canada, points out the basic flaws in this old wives' tale. "First of all, it is obvious that the brain, like all our other organs, has been shaped by natural selection." Furthermore, brain tissue is, as Beyerstein puts it, "metabolically expensive both to grow and to run." It boggles the mind to imagine that nature would have permitted the brain to develop into a massively underemployed organ.

Both Chuder and Beyerstein agree: we use 100% of our gray matter, though not necessarily all at once. Benjamin Radford, psychologist and editor of *The Skeptical Inquirer*, observes, "Just as people don't use all of their muscle groups at one time, they also don't use all of their brain at once."

If the common sense argument doesn't convince you, there is always the research of clinical neurologists. They have found that whether it is a stroke or a serious head injury, the brain suffers some kind of damage: there is no spare part of the brain that is immune to trauma, or can step in to help when other little gray cells can't carry the load any more. In the course of brain surgery, neurologists have directed electrical stimulation to every part of the brain. They did not find any areas that were dormant, just waiting for a chance to kick into high intellectual gear.

So where did this old wives' tale come from? Beyerstein thinks the late-19th/early-20th-century psychologist and philosopher William James (brother of the novelist Henry James) inadvertently popularized the 10 percent myth. Between his scholarly activities as a Harvard professor, James wrote articles for popular magazines urging readers to improve themselves. A common theme in these articles was that individuals rarely realize more than a small percentage of their real potential. James never mentioned a particular percentage, but the self-help, power-of-positive-thinking, motivational speakers who followed him began to claim that we were only using 10 percent of our potential. It was easy for such a claim to be restated as "10 percent of our brain." Finally, in his preface to the 1936 edition of Dale Carnegie's self-help blockbuster, *How to Win Friends and Influence People*, the celebrity journalist Lowell Thomas brought the claim full circle by attributing the "we're only using 10 percent of our brain" myth to William James.

"The 10-percent myth has undoubtedly motivated many people to strive for greater creativity and productivity in their lives," Beyerstein says. "Hardly a bad thing." But like so many old wives' tales, it is just too good to be true.

WE ARE TALLER THAN OUR ANCESTORS WERE

How True Is It?
This story actually measures up.

Visitors to historic homes often remark on how low the ceilings are, and how small the beds. (Mind you, we're talking the homes of ordinary folk, not Versailles.) Invariably, either a tourist or the tour guide will assert that a couple hundred years ago, people were shorter than they are today. The most common reason offered is nutrition: thanks to plentiful amounts of vitamin-rich food, we are giants when compared to our ancestors.

It seems to make sense, but when it comes to old wives' tales it is best to be skeptical. Nonetheless, Michael J. Dougherty, assistant director and senior staff biologist at Biological Sciences Curriculum Study in Colorado Springs, Colorado, says that "over the last 150 years the average height of people in industrialized nations has increased approximately 10 centimeters (about four inches)."

Why the dramatic increase? Geneticists believe that better nutrition, especially among children, has given our average height a boost. And the evidence does seem to support this idea. For example, from the first humans to the early 1800s, skeletal remains show virtually no change in the height of the average human. "Chronic underfeeding during childhood," Dougherty explains, "permanently affects stature." In other words, for thousands of years, most human children were not getting enough nutritious food in order to grow and develop. It is the chronic part that causes the trouble. A temporary disruption in nutrition can be overcome later. Dougherty cites the example of German children during World War I and World War II: food was hard to come by in those days, and children showed the effects of the food shortages by being slow to grow. After the wars were over, however, and food was plentiful again, the underdeveloped children of Germany recovered. According to Dougherty, "slow growth induced by temporary malnourishment can usually be reversed. Chronic underfeeding during childhood, however, permanently affects stature and other traits, including intelligence."

Does this mean humans will continue to grow ever taller until a seven-foot frame is the standard? The short answer is, "No."

"The trend toward increasing height has largely leveled off," Dougherty says, "suggesting that there is an upper limit to height beyond which our genes are not equipped to take us, regardless of environmental improvements."

PEOPLE WITH RED HAIR ARE TEMPERAMENTAL

How True Is It?
Just a stereotype.

You don't want to be a redhead in France. It's enough that red hair is taken as a sign of a short fuse and a sexually voracious appetite, but French old wives' tales insist that people with red hair are not to be trusted. The stigma is so widespread that redheaded French women have banded together to form an advocacy group known as Association Francaise des Rousses.

Where does red hair come from? It's the result of a recessive gene that tends to occur in people from Western Europe. About .03 percent of the French have red hair. Between 3 and 5 percent of Western Europeans and their descendants around the globe are redheads. That number rises to about 15 percent in certain Irish and Scottish towns that 1,200 years ago experienced frequent visits from the Vikings. But red hair has been known to turn up among Egyptians, Israelis, and even Nigerians.

In terms of folklore, different cultures have different takes on redheads. In Denmark a redheaded child is considered a blessing. In Corsica, you want to ward off a redhead just as you want to ward off the evil eye, while in Poland it's said that if you pass three redheads in the street, it's a sign that you will win the state lottery.

According to Harvard dermatologist Madhu Pathak, people with red hair have several strikes against them (and it's not the negatives the old wives talk about). Because redheads tend to have fair skin, they haven't enough pigment to filter out sun-

Famous Redheads

Judas Iscariot, betrayer of Jesus Christ (oral tradition, not the gospels, makes him a redhead)
Nero, Emperor of Rome and persecutor of Christians
Christopher Columbus, discoverer of the New World
Henry VIII, marriage-mad King of England
Mary Stuart, romantic Queen of Scotland
Rob Roy, celebrated Scots outlaw
George Washington, first president of the United States
Thomas Jefferson, author of the Declaration of Independence
Napoleon Bonaparte, megalomaniac Emperor of France
Vincent van Gogh, moody Impressionist painter
Lizzie Borden, alleged ax murderer
Maureen O'Hara, feisty Hollywood film actress
Woody Allen, neurotic New York comedian, actor, director
Nicole Kidman, A-list Hollywood film star

light, which makes them more susceptible to sunburn, skin cancer and wrinkles.

But the rest is fable (or fantasy): no study has ever proven that redheads have hotter tempers, or libidos, than their more-conventionally-colored counterparts.

WE'RE ONLY SIX DEGREES AWAY FROM EVERY OTHER PERSON ON THE PLANET

How True Is It?
Evidence is compelling, although not definitive.

It was the John Guare play and movie, *Six Degrees of Separation*, that popularized the otherwise obscure idea that all humankind is mysteriously linked together. The father of this old wives' tale was a Hungarian writer, Frigyes Karinthy. Back in 1929 he conjectured that there are only five intermediary individuals between you and everyone else on Earth. Karinthy's notion became known as the "Small World Problem," and his theory of linkages as "six degrees of separation."

The idea is appealing, in a sentimental kind of way. (Unless you're an isolationist, in which case it's downright scary.) But it wasn't until the 1950s that anyone tried to prove Karinthy's theory.

Manfred Kochen, a mathematician, and Ithiel de Sola Pool, a political scientist, tried to find a mathematical solution. They set forth the theory that if you were to choose 1000 friends at random from 100 million people, then any two individuals would be separated by only two or three degrees of separation. The Kochen-de Sola Pool method didn't hold water, however, because people do not choose their friends at random.

In the 1960s social psychologist Stanley Milgram and his graduate student Jeffrey Travers decided to test Karinthy's theory in a fresh way. They gave a letter to 300 individuals who lived either in Boston or Omaha. The letter was addressed to a stockbroker in Sharon, Massachusetts. Each person who received the letter was supposed to pass it on to someone he or she believed

Six Degrees of Kevin Bacon

Inspired by the John Guare play and movie, not to mention a little alcohol, in 1994 three Pennsylvania college students created a now-famous game: Six Degrees of Kevin Bacon. The students then appeared on a popular comedy television show. The rest, as they say, is history-and a website, book, and board game.

The students, Craig Fass, Brian Turtle, and Mike Ginelli, decided to use the actor Kevin Bacon to demonstrate that the world of actors is indeed small. Why Kevin Bacon, you ask? Well, the three young men must have learned something about scanning poetry from their English professors. His name contains the same number of syllables as the word "separation" and employs a similar rhythm. Try it: SEP-a-RA-tion. KEV-in BA-con. Bacon, they also reasoned, by virtue of having appeared in numerous ensemble films during the last two decades, could be linked to all other actors by no more than six degrees .

Try it out some time, using any actor you want. Start with this person and count the steps it takes you to get to Kevin Bacon. Once you get to six, however, you have to stop. Six Degrees of Kevin Bacon neither proves nor disproves theories about linkages. But it is a fun way to test your knowledge of movie trivia.

was closer to the target (as Milgram and Travers called the stockbroker). Of the 300 copies of the letter, 64 arrived in the stockbroker's mailbox. And on average, it took a chain of six people to get the letter to him. Hence the name for the theory, the phenomenon, the play, and the movie.

Writing in *Scientific American* magazine, Duncan J. Watts, an associate professor of sociology at Columbia University, and the principal investigator of the ongoing Small World Research Project, says Milgram and Travers' experiment is intriguing. But the matter has yet to be settled, and probably never will be: a definitive study would require surveying the whole of humanity.

SHAVE YOUR BODY HAIR AND IT WILL GROW BACK THICKER

How True Is It?
Not at all.

Swimmers and bodybuilders have long shaved their bodies. These days many ordinary guys remove their body hair so the world can enjoy an unobstructed view of their gym-built muscles. According to the old wives, however, once you shave your body, the hair will grow back thicker and maybe even darker than it was originally.

It sounds ominous. Or at least ironic. But it's not true. There are issues to consider before shaving your body, but the fear of being transformed from a masculine, moderately hairy guy into a shaggy gorilla is not among them.

The most common condition associated with shaving body hair is razor burn, a red, itchy skin irritation that is generally caused by dragging the razor too hard across the skin, or shaving the hairs against the grain. In some cases a razor can even infect the hair follicles. The act of shaving opens the follicles, making them susceptible to bacteria. Infected follicles, a condition known as Folliculitis, produce red bumps on the skin, which are both uncomfortable and unsightly. Generally an antibacterial soap will clear up the problem, but a more serious case in which the follicles fill up with pus requires a trip to the doctor.

There are many other hair-related myths. For example, the old wives assure us that brushing your hair one hundred times before going to bed will make it thick and lustrous. Nonsense. Excessive brushing can break healthy strands of hair, scratch your scalp, and pull out hair that your head wasn't yet ready to shed.

What about the claim that if you pull out one gray hair, two or more will grow in its place? It makes sense—but only if you believe in vengeful gray-hair gods. In fact this myth is rooted in a misconception about how hair grows. First, in most cases gray hair is a sign that you are aging. Once you pluck out a hair, it takes six months for a new one to fully grow in. By the time the plucked-out hair's replacement grows in, you're six months older, and chances are that you've acquired a few more gray hairs than you had on the day you performed the plucking.

The ubiquitous strands of hair curled up in just about everybody's shower drains have given birth to the notion that shampooing makes hair fall out. It simply isn't true. Shampooing has no effect on healthy hair. Our heads are sloughing off old dead hair all the time. The strands of hair that have collected in and around your drain were ready to drop off anyway—the act of washing just eased their passage.

Cosmetic companies have told us that we shouldn't trim off split ends, rather we should heal them by buying their miracle split-end restorative products. Baloney. Split ends can't be healed. They can be temporarily fused together by some kind of commercial goop. But once the goop is washed away, the split ends will reappear.

Extreme Fear Can Turn Your Hair White Overnight

It's said that the night before she went to the guillotine, Marie Antoinette was so terrified that between dusk and dawn her hair turned white. This old wives' tale about the power of fear or anxiety to whiten hair has enjoyed wide circulation for centuries. Marie Antoinette herself believed it. After she and the rest of the royal family failed to escape from France, she sent a lock of her hair to her closest friend, the Princesse de Lamballe, with a note saying, "Unhappiness turned it white."

The queen's biographer, Antonia Fraser, tells us that Marie Antoinette's hair had been going white (or at least gray) for years. Five years before she sent her token to the Princesse, a visitor to the French court, Count Esterhazy, noticed that Marie Antoinette was going gray. Before the French Revolution, when she had a small army of hairdressers powdering, pomading, and coloring her hair, the queen probably would not have noticed the gray. Once her troubles began and the hairdressers were no longer around to tend the royal coiffure, the white hairs suddenly would have become noticeable. In keeping with the old wives' tale, Marie Antoinette would have blamed her white hair on her sorrows, not her lack of access to hair dyes.

But there is another possibility: a condition called diffuse alopecia areata can cause sudden loss of dark or pigmented hair, leaving the white or gray hairs behind. Doctors haven't been able to pinpoint what biological conditions set off alopecia, but there is some evidence that a shock or emotional stress may contribute to it. This situation gives the impression that someone's hair has "turned white overnight."

Section Twelve

To Bring Good Luck, Knock on Wood, and Other Old Wives' Tales on How to Attract Good Luck and Avoid Bad Luck

TO BRING GOOD LUCK, KNOCK ON WOOD

How True Is It?
It doesn't have a prayer.

The ancient Celts were tree people: they regarded the oak, the ash, the holly, and the hawthorn as especially sacred, but they also believed that every tree had its own protective spirit that could do mankind good. If 2,000 years ago a Celtic chieftain announced to his tribe, "Tomorrow we're going to vanquish the Romans!" he would immediately knock on a tree, a door beam, or any other piece of wood so that the guardian spirit would emerge to make what the chieftain hoped for come true and drive away any evil spirits who might want to thwart the chief's plans.

A variation on this theme developed in Ireland. When someone in Ireland has experienced a bit of good luck, the tradition is to knock on wood to thank the little people who dwell there and made it all possible.

There are no statistics about the efficacy of knocking on wood. But we're willing to go out on a limb and state that it is unlikely that every tree, let alone every scrap of lumber, has a dryad just waiting to do good in the world.

The tradition of knocking on wood was so pervasive in the Celtic world that even after the Celts were converted to Christianity they still kept up this custom. The Church "baptized" it, as it were, by suggesting that knocking on wood was a harmless commemoration of the True Cross.

By the way, "knock on wood" is the American version. In the British Isles you say "touch wood."

BREAK A MIRROR AND YOU'LL HAVE SEVEN YEARS OF BAD LUCK

How True Is It?
It's nothing to worry about beyond the shards.

Nothing fills the old wives with horror quite like the sight of a shattered mirror. Two superstitions come together in this old wives' tale: the ancient notion that the mirror catches the reflection of the soul, and the ancient Roman belief that every person is essentially remade, body and soul, every seven years. And some New Age philosophers subscribe to a similar belief, contending that our cells regenerate every seven years.

Almost from the moment mirrors were invented (more than 4,000 years ago), people from Egypt to China to Mexico believed that the image they saw in the glass was not just a reflection of the human form, but also a glimpse of the individual's soul. This belief led to a host of precautionary measures. Mirrors were covered at night or during an illness because, some traditions held, the soul of a sleeping or sick person left the body and traipsed about the world. A restless soul, free from its body, would not see its reflection and become trapped for all eternity in the glass. At the moment of death, mirrors were covered or turned toward the wall so that the soul would not make the mistake of moving toward the mirror instead of heading for eternal life in the next world. Years ago in Bulgaria this tradition was followed with almost religious zeal because Bulgarians believed if the soul of the newly departed became trapped in a mirror, it would wait there to steal the soul of the next living person who looked into the glass.

This connection of the mirror and the soul led to one of the best-known bits of vampire folklore. A vampire has no reflection in a mirror because, as one of the undead, a vampire has no soul.

The ancient Greeks were nervous around reflective pools of water. They believed that in such places lived malignant spirits eager to steal the soul of whoever looked at their reflection on the surface of the water. With the soul gone, the body, of course, would die. A version of this Greek myth survived in the legend of mermaids who seized unwary sailors, dragging them to their deaths at the bottom of the sea.

Probably it was the ancient Romans who associated seven years of bad luck with a broken mirror. Since the mirror reflected the soul, a shattered mirror would cause serious damage to the soul of the individual who broke it. The Romans believed that the body and soul changed every seven years, and so concluded that seven years would pass before the harm done by the broken mirror would be repaired. To save time, however, the Romans said that if you ground the broken mirror to dust so small that no reflection could be seen, then the whole seven years of bad luck would be nullified. African-American slaves found an easier way to get rid of the bad luck: they picked up all the broken pieces of the mirror, set them in a stream running south, and left them there for seven hours—long enough for all the bad luck to be washed away.

CERTAIN LUCKY NUMBERS COME UP AGAIN AND AGAIN IN THE LOTTERY

How True Is It?
The odds are against it.

If experience teaches us anything, it is that working hard gets us nowhere. The best way to hit the Big Score is to win the lottery. According to the old wives—who, of course, have a foolproof system—there are certain winning numbers that appear time and again in the lottery.

And the old wives are right! For example, between January 1989 and June 2005, some numbers have been drawn more than others. The number 34 was the most frequently drawn, appearing 271 times (the choices range from 1 to 42). Number 9 has been a winning number 252 times, 10 has been drawn 249 times, 30 has come up 248 times, 12 has been among the winning numbers 247 times, followed closely by the numbers 2 and 17, which have been drawn 245 times.

Knowing which numbers turn up most often is useful, but what the lottery faithful really want to know is, how often do all six winning numbers repeat themselves? According to Colorado Lottery statisticians, the same six winning numbers will recur every 2700 drawings. Before you get excited, consider that Colorado holds only 104 drawings every year, so you'll have to wait 16 or 17 years before the winning six come back again.

English statisticians caused quite a stir when their findings indicated England's National Lottery might not be random. In their 2002 report entitled *The Randomness of the National Lottery*, Dr. John Haigh and Professor Charles Goldie, both members of the Royal Statistical Society, found that number 38 popped up among the winning numbers most often: in 637 games played between 1994 and 2002, lucky 38 was drawn 107 times. But in the December 16, 2004 issue of the English newspaper *The Guardian*, journalist David Adams offered readers the following advice: "Don't put your house on it." The 2002 report "may have suggested the number 38 ball be 'physically examined' because it was sucked out of the machine so often, but the 100 or so draws since have seen it fall back into the statistically normal pack. Plus, if there was a physical anomaly with the ball, it would have to be repeated in each of the eight possible sets used for the main Lotto draw, of which one is selected at random each week."

Haigh and Goldie's findings were, according to Adams, "a freak." But England's National Lottery Commission took them seriously enough to ask the University of Salford's Centre for the Study of Gambling for a second opinion. "All tests support the hypothesis of randomness," this think tank concluded. "That is, they confirm no evidence of nonrandomness among the Lotto draws."

In 1992, the Texas Lottery experienced a remarkable anomaly: number 23 had appeared in six out of eight drawings in a row.

Once you know which are the luckiest numbers, the next step is to find the luckiest lottery ticket vendor. Head to Australia and buy your ticket from the Lotto kiosk at the Garden City Lotto Lottery Centre: it has had 7 wins in 7 years.

Reading over these statistics, it's understandable if one were tempted to put one's faith in the power of certain winning numbers. Before you rush off and buy a pile of tickets, however, bear in mind that these results are based on anecdotal, random evidence. As Stephen Jay Gould writes in *Streak: Joe DiMaggio and the Summer of '41*, "The statistics of streaks and slumps"-or in our case, allegedly lucky numbers, "do teach an important lesson . . . about life in general. The history of a species, or any natural phenomenon that requires unbroken continuity in a world of trouble, works like a batting streak. All are games of a gambler playing with a limited stake against a house with infinite resources. The gambler must eventually go bust. His aim can only be to stick around as long as possible, to have some fun while he's at it, and, if he happens to be a moral agent as well, to worry about staying the course with honor."

The sobering truth is, every number has an equal chance of being selected on any given day. There is no magic formula for winning the lottery.

NUMBER 13 IS LUCKY OR UNLUCKY

How True Is It?
It has a reputation both ways, but no science on its side.

In virtually every part of the Christian world, old wives recoil at the number 13. It is not uncommon to find airliners that don't have a 13th row, or hotels that don't have a 13th floor. We'll explore the origins of this accursed number when we examine Friday the 13th, but for the moment, let's look at one group that regards 13 as lucky: the Greeks.

The way the Greeks see it, 13 represents Christ plus his twelve apostles. Seen in that light, how could such a number be bad? True, Greeks who have emigrated from their homeland, and their descendants, generally have adopted the more common phobia about number 13. But back in the Old Country, Greeks continue to regard 13 as a number top-heavy with good omens. And recently their faith in the inherent goodness of 13 was rewarded: at the Sydney Olympics in 2000, Greece had its best show ever, coming home with 13 gold medals.

NUMBER 8 IS LUCKY IN CHINA

How True Is It?
It hardly matters.

Doing everything to ensure good luck and avoid bad luck can be a full-time occupation in China—and not just among old wives. Even young computer geeks and international business moguls worry about such things.

Consider the number 8: in Chinese it is pronounced "ba," which is close to the Mandarin and Cantonese word "fa," which means "to prosper." As a result, 8 is the most auspicious and desirable of lucky numbers in Chinese culture.

How desirable? In August 2003, executives of Sichuan Airlines paid 2.33 million yuan (in U.S. dollars that's $288,000) in a special auction to secure 8888-8888 as the company's 24-hour customer service hotline. If one eight is good, eight eights all in a row must be exceptional. It is the equivalent of hitting the good luck jackpot. Xing Bing, a spokesperson for Sichuan Airlines, assured a reporter from the Associated Press, "Everyone at the company believes the number was worth the price we paid."

Chinese immigrants to the United States have brought their faith in lucky number eight with them. Realtors in California's San Gabriel Valley have learned that among Chinese house buyers, an eight in the address is perceived as value-added. And just like the executives of Sichuan Airlines, the Chinese immigrants will pay a premium for phone numbers, fax numbers, automobile license plates, and bank account numbers that carry a lot of eights. Flip through the

Chinese Yellow Pages for San Gabriel Valley, and the number eight is everywhere.

On the flip side, the numbers 4 and 14 are notoriously unlucky. It would be hard to find to a highrise in Beijing that lists a fourth or fourteenth floor in its directory. A Westerner who writes a regular column on life in China for the website www.pekingduck.org found out why most Chinese prefer to keep 4 and 14 at arm's length. After he had been assigned a new phone number that included the digits 14114, a friend explained to him that in Chinese "one" sounds like the verb "want" and "four" sounds like the word "die." To any Chinese calling him, the expatriate's new phone number read, "I want to die, I want, I want to die."

7 IS THE PERFECT NUMBER

How True Is It?
Hard data is hard to find—but not adherents.

Among Jews and Christians, Egyptians and Greeks, seafarers and motivational speakers, seven is the perfect number. It was the Pythagoreans, the disciples of the ancient Greek mathematician Pythagoras, who first applauded the perfection of seven because it was the sum of 3, which represents the triangle, and 4, which represents the square. And among the Pythagoreans, the triangle and the square were the two perfect geometrical forms.

Other ancient civilizations regarded seven as the number of perfection. The Babylonians believed the seven planets were arranged in levels on spheres of crystal, with the seventh planet existing on the highest level known as "seventh heaven"—an expression we still use for being in a place that couldn't possibly be any better. In the ruins of ancient Nineveh the archaeologist A.H. Layard (1817-1894) found clay tablets covered with charms, prayers, and incantations that were supposed to be recited seven times in order to work. Groups of seven occur at least 300 times in the Bible, one of the most famous being the formula that brought down the walls of Jericho. For seven days seven priests walked before the Ark of the Covenant, blowing seven ram's horns. On the seventh day they circled Jericho seven times. On the seventh circuit they blew their horns and the walls came tumbling down. And in ancient Ireland, a man was considered well-to-do if he possessed these seven things: a house, a mill, a kiln, a barn, a sheep pen, a shed for calves, and a pigsty.

No matter where you look in high culture or popular culture, you run into sevens. The Seven Days of the Week. The Seven Days of Creation. Seven Fat Years and Seven Lean Years. The Seven Gods of Egypt. The Seven Horses of Mithra. The Seven Wonders of the World. The Seven Wise Men of Greece. The Seven Hills of Rome. The Seven-Branched Menorah. The Seven Lucky Gods of Japan. The Seven Archangels. The Seven Sleepers of Ephesus. Seventh Heaven. The Seven Deadly Sins. The Seven Cardinal Virtues. The Seven Sorrows of the Virgin Mary. The Seven Chakras. The Seven Ancient Planets. The Seven Sisters Constellation. The Seven Seas. The Seven Ages of Man. The Seven Cities of Cibola. The Seven Colors of the Rainbow. The Amish Dinner of Seven Sweets and Seven Sours. The Seven-Year Itch. The Seven Dwarves. Seven Brides for Seven Brothers. The Seven Samurai. The Magnificent Seven. Trial of the Chicago Seven. T.E. Lawrence's *The Seven Pillars of Wisdom*. Stephen Covey's *7 Habits of Highly Effective People*.

You get the idea.

The Pythagorean rationale for why seven should be such a great number makes sense, but why it is regarded as an ideal number in virtually every corner of the world and in virtually every period of history remains impossible to pin down. It is enough to recognize that the appeal of the number seven is rooted deep in the human psyche, and who are we to question Nature?

TUESDAY IS UNLUCKY

How True Is It?
It has a certain history, but it is strictly superstition.

Throughout most of the Western world Friday is considered unlucky, but among the Greeks Tuesday is dreaded as the unluckiest day of the week. They have a good reason for this superstition: on Tuesday, May 29, 1453, Constantinople fell to the Turks, and the last Byzantine emperor, Constantine XI, died fighting in defense of his city. Two days of murder and rape, looting and sacrilege followed until the sultan, Mehmet the Conqueror, called an end to the orgy. The disaster marked the end of the Greek empire in the Eastern Mediterranean and the beginning of more than 400 years of near-slavery for the Greeks under the Turks.

Since 330, when the Emperor Constantine moved the imperial capital there from Rome, Constantinople had been a political and cultural dynamo. As Rome faded into a semi-deserted backwater, and while the rest of Europe was dealing with wave after wave of invading barbarian hordes and struggling through the Dark Ages, Constantinople enjoyed a long Golden Age of art, scholarship, and technology, not to mention considerable political muscle.

Although the conquest of their great city came as a tremendous shock to the Greeks, they should have seen it coming. The Byzantine Empire, which once stretched through Asia Minor to Egypt and across North Africa, had shrunk to a sliver of what is now Turkey, and the mainland and islands of Greece. Recognizing that their capital was no longer a going concern, many inhabitants of Constantinople emigrated elsewhere, with the result that large portions of the city were virtually uninhabited. The city's famous impregnable triple ring of defensive walls still stood, but were in a bad state of disrepair. And the promised help from the Christians of Western Europe never came. After enduring 54 days of assaults and relentless artillery bombardments by a Turkish army, Constantinople fell.

To this day Greeks consider it unlucky to start any new business venture or project on a Tuesday. Many Greeks will not even enter a new shop on a Tuesday. Which makes the "Tuesday is unlucky" old wives' tale a self-fulfilling prophecy.

A CAT ABOARD SHIP BRINGS GOOD LUCK

How True Is It?
The cat does have its uses.

Sailors are said to be the most superstitious people on the planet (although American professional baseball players could probably give them a run for their money). Given the danger and unpredictability of the sea, it's no wonder that sailors have a host of beliefs and routines said to ensure a safe voyage. While many of these nautical superstitions are questionable, the cat aboard ship at least has a practical purpose: it is nature's own exterminator of mice and rats.

But sailors have attributed other powers to the cat. If the ship's cat cried, the voyage would be rough. If the ship's cat was playful, the voyage would be successful, with good winds. If a cat walked toward a sailor, it meant good luck would come to him; if the cat started to approach the sailor then suddenly turned away, it meant the sailor could expect bad luck.

Some sailors believed that a cat possessed awesome powers. Make the ship's cat angry and it would raise a storm at sea by lashing its tail about. Although we wouldn't go so far as to suggest that the motion of a cat's tail influences the weather, it is true that cats are sensitive to low atmospheric pressure systems that produce stormy weather. If a ship's cat seems restless, there's a good chance a storm is brewing.

It's thought that cats were first domesticated in Egypt 4000 years ago to defend the country's grain supply against rodents. The ancient Egyptians came to hold the cat in such high esteem that eventually they worshipped a cat goddess named Bast.

About the year 900 B.C. the first domesticated cats probably arrived in Europe aboard the ships of Phoenician traders. Since then ships have carried the domestic cat to every corner of the world.

WEARING AN OPAL IS UNLUCKY UNLESS IT IS YOUR BIRTHSTONE

How True Is It?
Wear them without fear.

At least 1000 years ago old wives had convinced even educated persons that the opal was an unlucky stone. In the 11th century Bishop Marbode of Rennes damned opals as "the guardian of the thievish race." He was alluding to a superstition that an opal rendered the wearer invisible—which made the stone very popular among thieves, burglars, and even spies.

Not everyone was so negative about opals. The ancient Greeks thought the stone gave the wearer the ability to tell the future. The stone's myriad colors reminded the ancient Romans of a rainbow, so they carried it as a talisman that would bring them good luck. And the Arabs believed the opal must have fallen from heaven—it was their way of accounting for its beauty.

Still, the bad reputation the opal acquired in the Middle Ages hung on in the modern era. During the 19th century, many people believed only those individuals born in October could safely wear the opal, their month's birthstone. Although most of us probably do not worry about donning the fiery gem even if we do not have October birthdays, many contemporary jewelers take care to dispute any lingering fears we may still have about purchasing a piece of opal jewelry.

Australians have been working hard to dispel the slur against the opal. They tell the story of Harry Brukarz, a Sydney jeweler who specialized in opals. Throughout the 1940s and

1950s Brukarz won lottery after lottery. He attributed his extraordinary luck to his opals.

The opal has been very, very good to Australia. Some of the most magnificent opals in the world have been found there, including the 180-carat "Aurora Australis," the world's most valuable black opal, discovered in 1938 at Lightning Ridge. In 2005 this stone was appraised for AUD$1 million.

Leaving "Aurora Australis" in the dust is Olympic Australis, the largest gem opal ever found. In 1956 a miner working the famous "Eight Mile" opal field in Coober Pedy, New South Wales, found the stone 30 feet down. It weighs 17,000 carats and was valued in 2005 at AUD$2.5 million. The gem is of such extraordinary purity that jewelers believe at least 7,000 carats could be cut from the Olympic Australis. Since it is such a unique piece, however, it will remain intact.

Naturally these fabulous opals have passed through the hands of countless individuals who were not born in October. Yet no epidemic of tragedies have been reported.

IT'S GOOD LUCK TO HANG A HORSESHOE OVER THE DOOR OF A HOUSE

How True Is It?
The myth is widespread, but not well-founded.

Old wives in ancient Rome assured homeowners and shopkeepers that witches and evil spirits dreaded iron. A few iron nails tacked around a doorway were sure to keep a house or business free from malign influences. This idea merged with another old wives' tale, the belief that blacksmiths possessed magical powers. After all, they could take a lump of crude metal and turn it into a host of useful objects. Including, of course, iron horseshoes. That is how the horseshoe replaced the iron nail as a good-luck emblem over the doorway of a house.

Examples of trust in the power of the horseshoe can be found all across Europe and North America. In Northumberland in England, the horseshoe not only drove off bad luck, but also the number of nail holes in the shoes told an unmarried man or woman who found it in how many years he or she would marry. In the northernmost regions of Scotland it was said that a horseshoe should be set up between the homes of two quarreling neighbors to neutralize the curses they hurled at each other. Seafarers from Scandinavia kept a horseshoe onboard ship to ward off lightning, the horseshoe being a survival from the old pagan Norse practice of sacrificing a horse before any major endeavor to win the favor of the gods.

The one major point upon which old wives disagree is how to hang the horseshoe. In Germany and the United States the shoe hangs upwards so that the luck doesn't run out. In other parts of Europe, however, the horseshoe is hung pointing downward so the good luck will flow into the house.

Farriers, horse owners, and horseshoe pitchers apparently do not put much stock in this old wives' tale. Given how much time these people spend around horseshoes, they would probably be in the best position to benefit from any good luck the horseshoe had to offer. In reality, horseshoes have caused more than a few mishaps, usually because of human error, not bad luck.

Many horses have sustained serious injuries because they have been poorly shod. Many a farrier has been kicked by a dissatisfied horse. Horseshoes have been around for a long time. They make horses' lives easier and can be fun to play with. But they won't bring you good luck no matter how you hang them on your door.

FRIDAY THE 13TH IS UNLUCKY

How True Is It?
Well, it's certainly bad for business.

Whenever Friday the 13th rolls around on the calendar, you can count on virtually every radio and television newscaster to make some reference to it. It is the gold standard of old wives' tales, and perhaps their most successful (in terms of being one of the most widely held phobias).

Where does it come from? It is actually an unholy alliance of two separate terrors common in the Western world: fear of the number 13, and fear of Friday. Put these two together and you have very potent negative juju.

One reason for fear of 13 comes from the New Testament. There were 13 guests at the Last Supper, one of whom, Judas Iscariot, left the meal early to betray Jesus. As a corollary, this is the origin of the superstition that having 13 at table is bad luck.

You can also find an example of 13 as an ill-fated number in Norse mythology. At Valhalla, 12 gods were having a dinner party when in walked a thirteenth and uninvited god, the crafty Loki. True to his reputation as a troublemaker, Loki talked the gods into playing a silly party game: let's see if any missile can hurt Baldur the Beautiful, the god of joy, and the only god believed to be immune to all harm. Playfully, the gods threw one thing after another at Baldur, but nothing hurt him. Then Loki helped Hoder, the blind god of darkness, hurl a mistletoe-tipped dart at Baldur. Mistletoe was the one thing that could hurt Baldur. The dart struck, and Baldur fell dead. Instantly the whole Earth was plunged into darkness as nature went into mourning for Baldur.

Thomas Fernsler of the Mathematics and Science Education Resource Center at the University of Delaware explains that in almost all Western societies, 12 is regarded as a complete number. An even dozen is as good as it gets: 12 months in a year, 12 signs of the zodiac, 12 gods of Olympus, 12 tribes of Israel, and 12 apostles of Jesus. Add one more, and that once-tidy dozen is suddenly off-kilter.

Donald Dossey, founder of the Stress Management Center and Phobia Institute in Asheville, North Carolina, reports that fear of the number 13 shows up in places we wouldn't expect. More than 80 percent of high-rises lack a 13th floor. Many airports don't have a Gate 13. Rare is the hospital or hotel with a Room 13. In Florence, Italy, the people responsible for assigning house numbers got around the number 13 problem this way: the house between number 12 and number 14 is number 12 and a half.

So that accounts for the 13 part of this unlucky equation. As for the Friday part, its roots go back to the Bible, especially Good Friday, when Jesus Christ was crucified. Adam and Eve were expelled from the Garden of Eden on a Friday. Cain slew his brother Abel on a Friday. God cursed the builders of the Tower of Babel on a Friday. Noah's Flood began on a Friday. And Solomon's Temple was destroyed by the Babylonians on a Friday. Ever since, superstitious people have regarded Friday with suspicion. Over the years, popular traditions have sprung up that intensify Friday's reputation as a bad-luck day.

In ancient Rome, Friday was the day for executions. That was true in England, too, where Friday became known as Hangman's Day.

Sailors have routinely refused to put to sea on a Friday, saying it will jinx the voyage. There is a story that a century ago the British government, tired of being hamstrung one day a week by a superstition, decided to debunk the Friday phobia once and for all. They commissioned a new ship. Its keel was laid on a Friday. The ship was launched on a Friday. The crew was selected on a Friday. Her captain was an old seadog named Jim Friday. The ship was christened H.M.S. Friday. And she embarked on her maiden voyage on a Friday. The H.M.S. Friday was never heard from again.

It all sounds very colorful, but Friday the 13th is only truly bad news in the business community. Dossey says, "It's been estimated that $800 or $900 million is lost in business on this day because people will not fly or do business they would normally do." How can a myth cause so much money to be lost? Because, Dossey goes on to explain, between 17 and 21 million people just in the United States have a superstitious dread of Friday the 13th. They may reshuffle their schedule so no major decisions must be made on that day, they may call in sick, or they may succumb to a full-blown incapacitating panic attack.

And its not just business that shows the effects of Friday-the-13th phobia. In England on Friday the 13th, the number of people admitted to hospitals because of car accidents has been shown to rise about 52 percent, perhaps because so many drivers and pedestrians are on edge that day.

Richard Wiseman, a psychologist at the University of Hertfordshire in Hatfield, England, believes that the bad luck associated with Friday the 13th is a self-fulfilling prophecy. People who think of themselves as unlucky tend to be very nervous on Friday the 13th and therefore much more prone to accidents. Which, of course, just reinforces their belief that they are unlucky and Friday the 13th is their personal day of disaster.

Section Thirteen

Elephants Are Afraid of Mice, and Other Old Wives' Tales from the Animal Kingdom

ELEPHANTS ARE AFRAID OF MICE

How True Is It?
Only a tiny bit true.

There's a scene in the Walt Disney cartoon *Dumbo* in which some elephants are being mean to the little guy. A mouse marches in among the herd to stand up for Dumbo. Naturally, all the elephants panic in comically Disneyesque kinds of ways.

Disney didn't invent the story that elephants are afraid of mice; it only capitalized on something everybody knows to be true. But are the naturalist old wives right? Can a tiny mouse really panic a pachyderm?

It depends on the circumstances.

Generally speaking, elephants aren't afraid of anything. As the biggest land animal in the world, they have no natural predators except man. Since they are vegetarians with no need to stalk their prey, keen eyesight is not essential for elephants. In fact, they do not see very well, a characteristic which is compounded by the location of their eyes, situated as they are on the sides of the elephant's head rather than at the front. Consequently, if something tiny should dart rapidly around the elephant's feet, the poor creature is spooked and will start to stomp erratically to get away from, or maybe trample, whatever is down there. This rarely occurs in the wild, but in zoos and circuses it's not unusual for a mouse to get into an elephant's enclosure or stall. The captured elephant's response to the rodent is the likely source of this myth.

Thanks to old Tarzan movies, generations have grown up believing that an elephant, when it feels that death is approaching, heads for the elephant graveyard to die among the bones of its ancestors. In the movies, of course, rapacious, unscrupulous ivory hunters are always searching for the elephant graveyard, and it is up to Tarzan and his animal pals to fend off the looters. While it is a decent plot twist, there is no basis in nature for the story. No elephant graveyard has ever been found in Africa.

In India Hindus regard the elephant as a symbol of good luck. The elephant-headed Hindu god Ganesha is believed to be a divine remover of all kinds of obstacles; Hindus invoke him before they begin any new endeavor so that their efforts will be blessed with success.

Elephants do have one fear which they share with humans: both species are frightened when they encounter the bones of their own kind.

OSTRICHES BURY THEIR HEADS IN THE SAND

How True Is It?
It just looks that way.

The old wives' tale that an ostrich, when it sees something dangerous or unpleasant coming, buries its head in the sand, is so popular that it's become a modern metaphor for someone who'd rather ignore a problem than face it head on. It's not true, but there is a bit of basis for the myth.

According to the World Wildlife Fund, an ostrich—especially an ostrich guarding a nest—will lie outstretched on the ground when it sees danger approaching. But this is a camouflage technique, not a case of the ostrich being in a state of denial. Furthermore, it is the job of the male ostrich to build a nest for forthcoming offspring, and he does this by using his bill to dig a shallow trench. Taken together, these two aspects of ostrich behavior account for the head-in-the-sand idea.

In real life ostriches are anything but cowardly. They are aggressive with each other, giving one another short, hard pecks with their bills whenever they feel threatened, or if some other ostrich has invaded their turf. And there is something else that will set them off: ostrich farmers in Israel have found that a male and female ostrich must be of the same size if they are to mate. If two ostriches of different sizes are put in a pen together, they may try to hook up. But once they realize they can't get the job done, the ostriches attack each other.

THE MOST POISONOUS THING ON EARTH IS POLAR BEAR LIVER

How True Is It?
Well, it is pretty nasty stuff.

There are worse things you could eat than polar bear liver. But in terms of making you deathly ill, if not outright dead, the old wives are absolutely right: this stuff will do the job.

Word of the dangers of eating polar bear liver got back to Europe in 1596. Willem Barents, a Dutch explorer, and his men were exploring the Russian Arctic, searching for the Northwest Passage, the fabled water route to Asia. One day they shot and killed a polar bear for food. Several men who made the mistake of eating the liver died.

Polar bear liver is such a potent poison that just one bite will cause vomiting and dizziness. Eating a few ounces produces the hideous reaction of making the skin peel off, and then you die.

The Inuits who live in the Arctic have known since time out of mind about the dangers of polar bear liver. When hunters kill a bear, they bury the liver deep so that their dogs won't find it.

What made the bear's liver lethal remained a mystery until the 1940s. Then, two British biochemists studied polar bear liver and found it contained dangerous levels of vitamin A. Most of the animals polar bears hunt for food are rich in vitamin A. The polar bear needs this vitamin for the same reason people do: to maintain healthy eyesight, skin, bones, and hair. But, we don't have to worry as much about finding our next meal whereas the polar bear must store large amounts of vitamin A in case the bear doesn't come across a vitamin-rich tasty morsel in the near future. So nature has given the polar bear a high tolerance for large amounts of vitamin A. Then the animal's liver filters vitamin A from its bloodstream and preserves it for future use. However, our livers were not designed for the rigors of arctic life nor did nature intend for us to consume an entire seal in one sitting. Doing so would make us gluttons, not to mention sick. The polar bear, however, cannot be sure where his next seal will be coming from and is built to feast when he can.

By the way, the toxicity of polar bear liver is intensified if it is eaten with alcohol. So forget about washing down that polar-bear pate with a nice 1996 Rioja.

VAMPIRE BATS SUCK HUMAN BLOOD

How True Is It?
Only once in a while.

Humans have always found bats to be creepy. In the Bible's Book of Leviticus, God ranks bats among "unclean fowls" that Jews may not eat. Shakespeare's witches in Macbeth tossed a little "wool of bat" into their cauldron. And of course, once Bram Stoker's blood-chilling novel, *Dracula*, was published in 1897, any hope of rehabilitating the bat's reputation was finished.

In fairness, you can't blame humans for being squeamish about bats. The rat-like body. The pointy wings. The nasty, razor-sharp teeth. That unearthly squeaking sound. Their habitat in caves or mine shafts. This creature of the night is not likely to replace the dog as man's best friend.

The vampire bat is found in northern Mexico, Argentina and Chile, and on the islands of Trinidad and Margarita off the coast of Venezuela. It does indeed survive on blood. Flying about three feet off the ground, it hunts for prey, which includes wild animals, cows, horses, pigs, and, occasionally, humans.

Bats find a victim by using a type of vampirish radio wave. Out of its nose the hungry bat emits an ultra-high frequency sound. The sounds travels outward until it strikes a mammal, then bounces back to be picked up by the bat's ultra-sensitive ears. This enables the bat to zero in on its target.

Let's say that the bat has found a pig, curled up on the ground and sound asleep. The bat lands nearby and crawls or hops over to its prey. Heat sensors located in the bat's nose identify the capillaries where the blood lies close to the surface of the pig's skin. With its tongue and teeth the bat cleans the area where it intends to feed, then takes a bite from its prey, and begins to lap up—not suck—the blood. A chemical in the bat's saliva keeps the pig's blood from clotting. Once the bat has drunk its fill of blood (about two tablespoons), it is too heavy to fly. Like a drunk falling off a bar stool, the bat drops off its prey to hide in the underbrush until it has digested its meal. A vampire bat must feast on blood every two or three days, or it will die.

Although Dracula, in the novel and the movies, has linked vampire bats with Transylvania, Europeans did not discover these creatures until the 16th century. Vampire tales, on the other hand, began to surface in Eastern Europe during the Middle Ages. Vampire bats got their names because, like the legendary vampires who rose from the dead and sucked the blood of living human beings, they, too, drank blood.

Unlike the mythical creature for whom they are named, vampire bats, when they do decide to feed on humans, usually aim for an ankle or a toe, not the neck. Fatalities caused by vampire bites stem from rabies, not blood loss. Many vampire bats do indeed carry this deadly disease. And their numbers appear to be on the rise. In March 2004, 13 Brazilians died after being bitten by rabies-carrying vampire bats. Brazilian health ministry officials speculated that deforestation and the availability of more livestock may have led to changes in the vampire bats' migratory patterns and increased their populations, possibly causing them to become more aggressive.

These bloodthirsty creatures do pose a threat to people in Central and South America. According to the Smithsonian Institution, efforts to reduce the number of vampire bats in this area of the world began in 1968, when deaths among cattle bitten by rabid vampire bats became a serious economic threat. The old wives' tales about vampire bats' danger to human beings remain the stuff of medieval legend and Bram Stoker's imagination. But if you live in Central or South American, make sure you and your animals keep rabies vaccinations current.

BEES AND WASPS SENSE FEAR

How True Is It?
True—in a manner of speaking.

When suddenly confronted by a swarm of bees or wasps, the old wives advise acting brave and standing absolutely still. Why? Because when bees and wasps sense fear, they attack.

Nature has not outfitted bees and wasps with fear-tracking radar, but it has given them the sense to recognize potentially threatening behavior. Remember that bees are programmed to protect the queen and the hive from intruders. If you inadvertently come near a hive, and then start hopping and flailing about in the usual manner of a human in the presence of bees, the bees are bound to interpret your actions as provocative. To make you go away, they will sting you.

Two other physical reactions are common among bee-phobic humans: we hyperventilate, and we break out in a sweat. According to U.S. Department of Agriculture entomologist Justin Schmidt, "If you're frightened, you exhale more CO_2, and the odors of your sweat become more pungent." Bees pick this up and become agitated because, as Schmidt goes on to say, "Bees are one thousand times more sensitive to certain chemicals than we are."

So bees can certainly identify the telltale signs that we are scared of them.

To get away from garden-variety bees and wasps, move very slowly. Chances are decent that you'll escape unstung.

Contrary to popular belief, you don't have to travel to southern Africa to meet a swarm of killer bees, or Africanized

Honeybees to use their formal name. They now live in southern Texas, New Mexico, and California as well as in Mexico, Central and South America. Unfortunately, killer bees look very much like other honeybees, so if you encounter a bee in one of these places, don't wait to find out where its ancestors hail from. Assume the worst, then move away and hold your breath—remember that carbon dioxide sets bees off. If a killer bee does sting you, however, then by all means panic and run very, very fast. Along with the pain of a killer bee's sting comes a pheromone that identifies you as a target for the rest of the hive. Killer bee stings are potentially life-threatening because you're likely to suffer multiple stings if you get too close to a colony of these aggressive, territorial, honey-producing insects. They don't want you around. They will chase you away and sting you if they can. So be cautious—but don't let the killer bees know you're afraid.

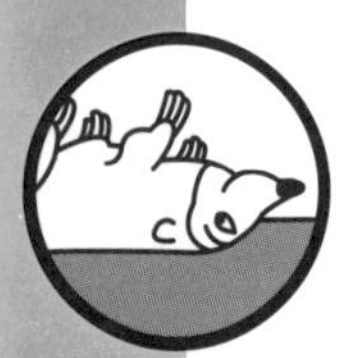

OPOSSUMS PLAY DEAD TO FOOL PREDATORS

How True Is It?
100 percent true.

To "play possum" is an American colloquialism for someone or something that is pretending to be what it isn't. Old wives tell lots of stories about animals that aren't true, but how about this one? Do opossums play dead so a predator will leave them alone?

The answer is yes. If you ever have a chance to grab a real, live opossum, you'll see the critter go catatonic instantly and assume the road-kill position: body curled, eyes blank, little claws turned inward like a half-formed fist. For the sake of realism, the "dead" possum drools from its mouth and releases nasty smelling green fluid from its anal glands. It's not only looks dead, it's disgusting to be around.

The act is absolutely convincing. Alfred L. Gardiner, curator of mammals for the National Biological Survey says, "You can freely handle [catatonic opossums], and even touch their eyeballs, and there's no reflex whatsoever." Gardiner goes on to say that in this state the opossum will not even respond to pain.

By some quirky plan of nature, opossums don't play dead when a predator is coming; instead, they wait until they are caught. By putting on a mighty convincing imitation of carrion (the stinky green slime oozing out the rear is a nice touch), the opossum manages to convince more than a few carnivores that he is not worth eating—and may even be dangerous to consume. The number of mauled but still alive opossums that dedicated possum-watchers have seen in the wild suggest that the tactic works.

LEMMINGS COMMIT MASS SUICIDE

How True Is It?
You can't be serious.

Since 1958 old wives have been stating with absolute certainty that, periodically, lemmings commit mass suicide by running to the edge of a cliff and hurling themselves into the sea. It's an indisputable fact. After all, they saw it in a movie called *White Wilderness*, part of the Disney studio's True Life Adventure series. The scene of the little critters jumping off the cliff was so vivid that even the *American Heritage Dictionary* defines a lemming as a rodent "noted for its mass migrations into the sea."

Disney and the dictionary—can you get two more reliable sources than that?

Well, yes, you can. The Canadian Broadcasting Corporation, for one.

In 1983 CBC producer Brian Vallee, tipped off by wildlife biologists that lemmings do not possess a self-destruct gene, began to investigate the Disney film. Vallee found that the mass suicide scene was faked. The Disney filmmakers bought a few dozen lemmings from Inuits in Manitoba; by using tight camera angles they created the impression of a horde of hysterical lemmings running across a snow-covered landscape toward their doom.

The film does show lemmings falling through the air and drowning in the water. But those scenes were faked, too. The movie was made in Alberta, a land-locked province of Canada. So the filmmakers chose for their location a cliff above a river. Again, tight camera angles enabled them to create the impression that the river was actually the ocean. As for the hurling part—it was members of the film crew who threw the animals off the cliff.

It's a damning story, but Alaska state wildlife biologist Thomas McDonough is willing to cut Disney a little slack. "Disney had to have gotten that idea from somewhere," he says. And McDonough believes he knows the source: Disney mistook the lemmings' habit of mass dispersal for self-destruction.

Lemmings are small rodents, related to voles. Their population in the wild fluctuates depending on predators and food supply. If they find themselves in a place with few predators and lots to eat, a lemming population can increase in size ten times in just one year. Once the food supply is gone, however, the lemmings disperse en masse to look for a new habitat. (By the way, moose and beaver do the same thing.) Zoologist Gordon Jarrell, an expert in small mammals with the University of Alaska Fairbanks, says that in Scandinavia hordes of lemmings have been observed backed up at a river or some other body of water. Lemmings can swim, but in such a pile-up quite a few lemmings will drown. That appears to be the source of the myth and the movie.

BIBLIOGRAPHY

Books

Browning, Robert, *A History of Golf, the Royal and Ancient Game*, (Dutton, 1955)

Daniels, Cora Linn and C.M. Stevens, editors, *Encyclopedia of Superstitions, Folklore, and the Occult Sciences of the World*, 3 volumes, (Gale Research Co., 1971)

Evans, Bergen, *The Natural History of Nonsense*, (Vintage Books, 1958)

Ferm, Vergilius Ture Anselm, *A Brief Dictionary of American Superstitions* (Oxford University Press, 1989)

Fraser, Antonia, *Marie Antoinette: The Journey* (Doubleday, 2001)

Michael, Robert T., et al., *Sex in America; A Definitive Survey*, (Warner Books, 1994)

Opie, Iona and Moira Tatem, editors, *A Dictionary of Superstitions* (Oxford University Press, 1989)

Radford, Edwin, *Encyclopedia of Superstitions* (Dufour Editions, 1969)

Rupp, Rebecca, *Weather!* (Storey Books, 2003)

Shermer, Michael, *Why People Believe Weird Things: Pseudoscience, Superstition, And Other Confusions Of Our Time*, (W.H. Freeman, 1997)

Sides, Hampton, editor, *Why Moths Hate Thomas Edison and Other Urgent Inquiries into the Odd Nature of Nature* (W.W. Norton, 2001)

Simons, G.L., *Sex and Superstition* (Barnes & Noble, 1973)

Simpson, J and S. Roud, *Oxford Dictionary of English Folklore* (Oxford University Press, 2000)

Tierno, Philip, *The Secret Life of Germs*, (Pocket Books, 2001)

Villiers, Elizabeth, illustrated by Victoria Hayatt, *The Book of Charms* (Simon and Schuster, 1973)

Walker, Morton, *The Power of Color*, (Avery Publishing Group, 1991)

Ward, Fred, *Opals* (Gem Book Publishers, 1997).

Articles

"Alkaloid turns spud green: Think what it can do to us!" by Jack Kerrigan, *Plain Dealer* (Cleveland, Ohio), December 23, 2000

"A new take on old wives' tales," *Courier Mail* (Queensland, Australia), April 13, 2004

"Appetite for a baby boy," by Fay Burstin, *The Daily Telegraph* (Sydney, Australia), June 30, 2003

"An Apple A Day Also Helps Brain; Might Lower Risk Of Alzheimer's," by Sharon Lem, *The Toronto Sun*, November 29, 2004

"Apple a day may keep cancer at bay," by Masaharu Asaba, *The Daily Yomiuri* (Tokyo), October 22, 2004

"Apple for sanity," by Syida Lizta Amirul Ihsan, *New Straits Times* (Malaysia), December 28, 2004

" Artificial Spider Silk Could Be Used for Armor, More," by Brian Handwerk for *National Geographic Channel*, January 14, 2005

"Ask Dr. Knowledge," The Boston Globe, January 22, 2004.

"Beware of the dog during a full moon, by Celia Hall, *The Daily Telegraph* (London), December 22, 2000

"Birthmarks, paper cuts: Not just skin deep," *The Straits Times* (Singapore), June 12, 2004

"Body and Mind: Curiosities are mostly an accident of birth," by Thomas Barlow, *Financial Times* (London,England), December 16, 2000

"The Cabbage Soup Diet; Why, Oh Why, Do People Keep Falling for It? Well . . .," by Judith Weinraub, *The Washington Post*, February 21, 1996

"Can shoe size predict penile length?" by J. Shah and N. Christopher, *British Journal of Urology International*, Volume 90 Issue 6, October 2002

"Celery Doesn't Have 'Negative Calories,' but Lots of Positives," by Sheldon Margen and Dale A. Ogar, *Los Angeles Times*, October 7, 2002

"Chicken soup is medicine, U.S. scientists confirm," *Reuters*, October 17, 2000

"Chills . . . and thrills," by Elaine Reeves, *The Mercury* (Australia), August 4, 2004

"Clear answers keep an eye on vision trouble," *The Atlanta Journal and Constitution*, March 6, 1996

"Clubbers risk losing the sound of silence," by Ian Murray, *The Times* (London), August 3, 1999

"'Cold hands, warm heart': Adage about women is true, researchers find," by Richard Starnes, *The Gazette* (Montreal, Quebec), June 6, 1998

"Coping with Unwanted Hair," by Deborah Blumenthal, *The New York Times*, May 22, 1983

"Cut the caffeine," by Manveet Kaur, *New Straits Times* (Malaysia), May 16, 2002

"Dairy Products Given Green Light: Milk Is Not A Liquid To Avoid If You Have The Stomach Flu, by Shelly Decker, *The Toronto Sun*, March 28, 2002

"Death Takes A Holiday: Forget the myth — this is a season of cheer, not suicide," by Lenore Skenazy, *Daily News* (New York), November 28, 2004

"Debunking the 'Day of Dread' for Women," by Ken Ringle, *The Washington Post*, January 31, 1993

"The Diet-Myth Grapevine: Two Wellness Experts Set The Record Straight On Some Food And Nutritional Untruths," by Sheldon Margen and Dale A. Ogar, *Orlando Sentinel* (Florida), March 11, 1999

"Difficult labour? It must be a baby boy," by Helen Puttick, *The Herald* (Glasgow), January 17, 2003

"Does Dim Light Affect Eyesight?" *Orlando Sentinel* (Florida), September 1, 1991

"Dogs Adored While Being Eaten in Seoul," by Bum-Jun Suh, *The Seoul Times*, 2005

"Dog's mouth wasn't sterile," *Fort Worth Star-Telegram* (Texas), January 12, 1996

"Eat It and Weep? Is 5-Second Rule Safe?" by Dru Sefton, Dru, *The Houston Chronicle* (Texas), September 29,

"The Ergogenic Effects Of Eurycoma Longifolia Jack: A Pilot Study," by S. Hamzah, A. Yusof, Department of Exercise Physiology, Sports Centre, University of Malaya, 2003

"Facing the (loud) music: Concert-goers, clubbers and ravers risk hearing loss," by Michelle Rainer, *The Gazette* (Montreal, Quebec), May 6, 2001

"Facts about cricket insects," by Christina VanGinkel, www.PageWise.com, Inc, 2002

"Fatty fish acid needed by fetuses, infants, nutrition experts say," by Leslie Papp, *The Toronto Star*, December 8, 1995

"Female fertility is all in the shape," by Tim Utton, *Herald Sun* (Melbourne, Australia), May 6, 2004

"File Theory Of Negative Calories Under 'We Wish'," *Buffalo News* (New York), January 8, 2002

"Finger of Suspicion: The state of your nails can be a good indicator of your health," by Stephanie Hirsch-Miller, *The Guardian* (London), October 27, 2001

"Folk Remedies Loom Large As Due Date Nears," by Eileen Dempsey, *Columbus Dispatch* (Ohio), May 10, 2002

"For your hearing's sake—turn it down," by Emma Horton, *The Independent* (London), April 7, 1998

"Foretelling a baby's sex with folklore: Oddly, your guess might not be as good as that old wives' tale," by Olivia Barker, *USA Today*, December 28, 1999

"Friday the 13th," by John Bowen, *Salon*, August 13, 1999

"Friday the 13th Phobia Rooted in Ancient History," by John Roach, *National Geographic New*, August 12, 2004

"'Full-Moon Effect' Lacks Proof," by Tom Burns, *The Columbus Dispatch*, June 9, 2002

"Full moon: that can mean only one thing Trust me... I'm a junior doctor," by Max Pemberton, *The Daily Telegraph* (London), November 05, 2004

"Full moon theories can be murder: Police, coroners put spin on old wives' tale," by Mike Weiss, *The San Francisco Chronicle*, March 2, 2002

"The future's auburn... and the word's spreading," *The Montreal Gazette*, August 31 2001.

"Getting past a few green potatoes," by Cathy Barber, *The Dallas Morning News*, March 1, 2000

"A Glass a Day: Cider has many of the apple's health benefits, and now's the time to enjoy it," by Ramin Ganeshram, *Newsday* (New York), October 1, 2003

"Hair Myths Get the Brush-Off," *St. Petersburg Times* (Florida), January 8, 1990

"Hallo Vera: Meet the plant that soothes burns, relieves pain and could one day save you," *The Straits Times* (Singapore), August 28, 2004

"Holiday Clubbers To Be Given Earplugs," by Matthew Beard, *The Independent* (London), August 16, 2003

"Home Cures Are Going Strong: More People Are Believers—Even Doctors Acknowledge The Benefits," *Orlando Sentinel* (Florida), February 1, 1998

"If Misfortune Blights Your Troth, Are You Protected?" by Melanie Bien, *Independent on Sunday* (London), May 23, 2004

"If you aren't born lucky, no amount of rabbits' feet will make a jot of difference," by Tim Radford, *The Guardian* (London), March 18, 2003

"Improving sex: Root vs horn: Early results show men being more virile after taking tongkat ali and Malaysia now plans on bigger trial, says doctor," by Sharmilpal Kaur, *The Straits Times* (Singapore), November 16, 2002

"In a glass of red wine, the health benefits may be many," by Deborah Scoblionkov, *Philadelphia Inquirer*, July 17, 2003

"In Eternal Search Of Elusive Love Potions," by Susan M. Barbieri, *Orlando Sentinel* (Florida), October 29, 1991

"In the lottery, all bets are off for number 23," by Stefanie Asin, *The Houston Chronicle* (Texas), December 31, 1992

"Is Friday the 13th Bad for Your Health?"by T.J. Scanlon, et al. *British Medical Journal*, December 18-25, 1993

"Is red wine good for you? Stick to an apple a day," by Joe Schwarcz, *The Gazette* (Montreal), December 19, 2004

"It's magpie season again," National Parks Media Release Archive, October 7, 2002

"It's Time To Salute Celery; The Crunchy Vegetable Is A Good Source Of Vitamin C, Fiber And Potassium," *Orlando Sentinel* (Florida), September 30, 1993

"Knuckle trouble," by Olivia Timbs, *The Independent* (London), July 10, 1990

"The Lean Plate Club: Positively Bunk," *The Washington Post*, October 30, 2001

"Let's clear the air about bad breath—It can be a serious health issue, not just a social complaint," by Mike Foley, *The Greenville News*, November 23, 2004

"Log Kept, Police Say - 'Obituary' Thefts Charted Carefully in 'Black Book'," *Los Angeles Times*, November 30, 1996.

"Looking for a Libido Lift? The Facts About Aphrodisiacs," by Tamar Nordenberg, *FDA Consumer* magazine, January-February 1996

"Man pleads guilty in aloe case: He accepts charge he distributed drug with intent to defraud: Treated over 3,000 people," by Jason Song, *The Baltimore Sun*, September 22, 2001

"Mood food," by Debra Taylor, *Sunday Mail Magazine* (Queensland, Australia), December 26, 2004

"Nails point a finger at medical problems," by Lila Lazurus, *The Detroit News*, May 26, 2004

"New analysis reveals human mouth carries more germs than expected," by Kristin Weidenbach, Media Release, Stanford University School of Medicine, December 8, 1999

"New rules let vintners tout wine's health benefit," by LISA MUNOZ, *The Orange County Register*, March 4, 2003

"Offensive Korean diet," *Shanghai Star*, November 15, 2001

"Penis size 'not linked to feet'," *BBC*, October 2, 2002

"People using home remedies to battle common ailments," by Barbara Isaacs, *The Toronto Star*, January 23, 1998

"Personal Health: Sucking thumbs," by Jane E. Brody, *The New York Times*, June 23, 1993

"PETA targets Korean dog meat: Caged protesters demand end to 'barbaric' practice," by Richard Starnes, *Ottawa Citizen* (Canada), May 31, 2002

"Poison Green Potatoes Have Seen The Light," by D. Williams, *Telegraph*, July 15, 1987

"Potatoes: One Thing That Should Be Kept In The Dark," *Courier-Mail*, December 12, 1990

"The pulse —The latest medical research from around the world," *The Weekend Australian*, November 15, 2003

"The pulse —The latest medical research from around the world," *The Weekend Australian*, November 20, 2004

"Quantum theory offers a chance at mind over matter: Brainpower could sink the shot or kill the cat," by Dan Vergano, *USA Today*, May 3, 2000

"Raise fertility chances with the food of love," by Paula Mee, *The Irish Times*, May 11, 2004

"Rap sheet on full moon has flaws," by Kevin O'Neal, *The Indianapolis Star*, July 12, 2003

"Reagan Suffers Mild Case Of Upset Stomach," by James Gerstenzang, *Los Angeles Times*, January 14, 1988

"Researchers Develop White Wine With Cholesterol-Lowering Benefits, Discover Israeli Wines Healthier Than French Wines," American Society For Technion, Israel Institute Of Technology, April 26, 2001

"Researchers say caffeine won't endanger pregnancy," by Amanda Husted and Rebecca Perl, *The Atlanta Journal and Constitution*, February 3, 1993

"Sacred heart to mistletoe tradition," *The Nelson Mail* (New Zealand), December 24, 2004

"Same 6 Lotto Numbers Repeat Every 2,700 Drawings," by Rebecca Jones, *Rocky Mountain News* (Denver, CO), February 1, 1998

"Scientific proof for tongkat ali," by Serge Kreutz, *Asia Daily*, November 2004

"Seafood great fix for brain," *Hobart Mercury* (Australia), July 17, 2002

"Seafood-deficient diet linked to depression," *Courier Mail* (Queensland, Australia), July 17, 2002

"Sex selection, the natural way," by Judith Woods, *The Daily Telegraph* (London), November 18, 2003

"Sole food is a good idea: Traditional belief that fish can benefit your brain has plenty of modern scientific backing," by Joe Schwarcz, *The Gazette* (Montreal, Quebec)

"Some facts about red-haired people," Globe and Mail, September 1, 1993.

"Some Holiday Plants Are Dangerous To Pets, Kids: Cyclamen, Amaryllis And Mistletoe All Fall Into The 'Toxic' Category," by Denise Cowie, *Charlotte Observer* (North Carolina), December 26, 2002

"Some Wives' Tales Withstand Scrutiny," by Marian Burros, *The New York Times*, February 23, 1994

"Spider Solidarity Forever: Social spiders create the communes of the arachnid world," by Laura Helmuth, *The Weekly Newsmagazine of Science*, Volume 155, Number 19 (May 8, 1999)

"Spoilt generation of little emperors rules the roost," by Ella Lee, *South China Morning Post* (Hong Kong), April 7, 2002

"State fines T-UP millions; Company also facing federal trial in sale of aloe vera as treatment," by Gail Gibson, *The Baltimore Sun*, May 11, 2000

"Stigma or Superstition? Appraisers Weigh Diminished Value of Tainted Properties," by Carole Fleck, realtors.org

"Stressed Out: April, Not December, Called Leading Month For Suicides," by John Schieszer, *St. Louis Post-Dispatch* (Missouri), December 29, 1996

"Suicide statistics," *The Straits Times* (Singapore), April 4, 2004

"Superstitions help players deal with frequent failure," by Ryan Clark, *Orlando Sentinel* (Florida), March 30, 2003

"Survey Asks: Do Men Have One Less Rib Than Women; Did Adam And Eve Have Navels?" *PRNewswire*, February 17, 2004

"A symbol of love: Mistletoe has other legendary powers," by Penny Reed, *Ottawa Citizen*, December 18, 2004

"Take a fish booster," *The Business Times Singapore*, August 2, 2002
"There's No Reason To Knock Off Knuckle- Cracking," by Rosie Mestel, *Los Angeles Times*, May 22, 2000
"Turning a deaf ear," by Donna Halvorsen, *Star Tribune* (Minneapolis, MN), August 5, 2003
"Virus Can Cause Warts," by Dr. Paul Donohue, *Sun-Sentinel* (Fort Lauderdale, FL), January 4, 1995
"What's in the Bottle? For quercetin, try an apple a day instead," *Newsday* (New York), November 30, 2004
"When it is hot, go herbal," by Li Xueying, *The Straits Times* (Singapore), May 3, 1998
"White is the new red," by Mark Henderson, *The Times* (London), June 7, 2001
"With This Insurance Policy, I Thee Wed ...," by Lindsey Rogerson, *The Scotsman*, April 10, 2004
"Women say dreams, feelings reveal baby's sex: Best guessers eschew folk methods, study says," by Jonathan Bor, *The Dallas Morning News*, September 5, 1999
"Women: The victims of St Valentine's Day," by Jane Sullivan, *The Guardian* (London), October 16, 1990
"Would you put your mouth here to save a life? With 4 hours of training, owners stand ready to perform CPR on furry friends," by Robert Davis, *USA Today*, July 26, 2000
"'You'll Catch Your Death!' An Old Wives' Tale? Well . . .," by Abigail Zuger, *The New York Times*, March 4, 2003
"You thought it was a lot of balls, but there's one you can count on," by Jamie Doward, *The Observer* (UK), December 12, 2004

Websites

afgen.com/china8.html
bss.sfsu.edu/geog/bholzman/courses/fall99projects/vampire.htm
chineseculture.about.com/library/weekly/aa081000a.htm
The Electronic Textbook of Dermatology, by Mark Naylor, M.D.
www.telemedicine.org/warts/cutmanhpv.htm
Holisticonline.com
insectzoo.msstate.edu/Students/orthoptera.html
itotd.com/index.alt?ArticleID=448
news.bbc.co.uk/1/hi/world/asia-pacific/3163951.stm
pekingduck.org/archives/000174.php
pekingduck.org/archives/000401.php
SnowCrystals.com
udayton.edu
wvlightning.com
www.answerbag.com/q_view.php/9847
www.answerbag.com/q_view.php/10420
www.babyhopes.com
www.bloodhoundclub.co.uk/History/10.htm

www.bridestuff.com
www.coolquiz.com/trivia/explain/docs/rice.asp
www.dentalcomfortzone
www.familymatters.tv
www.geocities.com/CapeCanaveral/3403/okfacts.html
www.insects.org/ced3/chinese_crcul.html
www.iowapoison.com
www.jorbins.com/gardening-magazine/articles/ladybug-garden.php
www.ladybuglady.com
www.lectlaw.com/def2/0021.htm
www.malereproduction.com
www.metaphor.dk/guillotine
www.moggies.co.uk/html/shipcat.html
www.mothernature.com
www.mypetstop.com
www.mystical-www.co.uk
www.newadvent.org
www.northshoregeneralpediatrics.com
www.obsidianmagazine.com/Pages/mirror.html
www.opalsdownunder.com.au
www.redandproud.com
www.sciam.com
www.scienceshorts.com/030404.htm
www.seniormag.com/caregiverresources/articles/halitosis.htmalitosis
www.sfu.ca/vpresearch/rm/bees.html
www.skeptics.com.au/journal/cricket.htm
www.straightdope.com/classics/a5_087.html
www.straightdope.com/mailbag/mostrich.html
www.ucar.edu/communications/infopack/lightning/kids.html
www.uic.edu/com/eye/LearningAboutVision/EyeFacts/CrossedEyes.shtml
www.wildlifenews.alaska.gov/
www.womenshealth.org/a/hot_tub_safety.htm
www.zoo.org/educate/fact_sheets/night/vmp_bat.html